THE ORDINATION OF EXEMPT RELIGIOUS

A History and a Commentary

THE CATHOLIC UNIVERSITY OF AMERICA
CANON LAW STUDIES
No. 271

The Ordination of Exempt Religious

A History and a Commentary

A DISSERTATION

SUBMITTED TO THE FACULTY OF THE SCHOOL OF CANON LAW OF THE CATHOLIC UNIVERSITY OF AMERICA IN PARTIAL FULFILLMENT OF THE REQUIREMENTS FOR THE DEGREE OF DOCTOR OF CANON LAW

BY

MAUR J. DLOUHY, O.S.B., A.B., J.C.L.
MONK OF ST. PROCOPIUS ABBEY

THE CATHOLIC UNIVERSITY OF AMERICA PRESS
WASHINGTON, D. C.
1955

NIHIL OBSTAT:

WENCESLAUS MICHALICKA, O.S.B., J.C.D.

Censor Deputatus

IMPRIMI POTEST:

✠AMBROSE ONDRAK, O.S.B.

Abbot of St. Procopius Abbey

IMPRIMATUR

✠MARTIN D. MCNAMARA

Bishop of Joliet-in-Illinois

20 January 1955

MURRAY AND HEISTER
WASHINGTON, D. C.

PRINTED BY
TIMES AND NEWS PUBLISHING CO.
GETTYSBURG, PA., U. S. A.

SUMMO ET AETERNO
SACERDOTI

TABLE OF CONTENTS

TABLE OF CONTENTS (Continued)

FOREWORD

While the discipline for the ordination of exempt religious has usually been considered as an exception to the general law, it can more easily be understood if accepted as an integrated parallel discipline. The changes introduced by the Code of Canon Law, while not radical, are sufficiently important to warrant special study. Most monographs which treat of the several requirements for ordination ordinarily indicate the variations involved in regard to exempt religious. Yet the entire process of ordination has not been treated as a unit. Perhaps this is due to the attitude, as expressed by a renowned canonist:

> Haec omnia statuta Codicis Iuris Canonici tam clara sunt, ut nulla explicatione indigeant.

No special effort has been made to treat of the matter of each requirement, but rather attention has been given to the integration of the canonical requisites with the nature of the religious state. The modifications in relationships which are occasioned by the operations of the three principals involved in the ordination of exempt religious—as contrasted with but two when secular clerics are promoted—are the primary matters for discussion.

The writer wishes to express his gratitude and appreciation to his Abbot and Community of St. Procopius Abbey and to the Faculty of the School of Canon Law of The Catholic University of America for providing the occasion for, as well as encouragement and assistance in the prosecution of his study of this phase of Canon Law.

21 March 1948
Washington, D. C.

CHAPTER I

Introduction

Although there is but one Priesthood of Jesus Christ to which all priests are configured, there exists a difference in the discipline according to which seculars and exempt religious are promoted to orders. In many matters the requirements are identical; in others a different but parallel procedure is provided; some few items are characteristic of the particular discipline.

Both seculars and religious may be promoted to the priesthood. Not only does the present law of the Church recognize and admit ordination in both classes,[1] but also provides the discipline according to which orders are conferred.[2] Moreover, history records both the fact that religious were ordained and the development of the alternate discipline for their ordination.

A. Historical Note

The evangelical counsels were observed by some of the early Christians. This ascetic manner of life was undertaken without a formal act of profession, though in some cases with some ceremony of dedication.[3] In organized religious life, which first flourished in the deserts of Egypt towards the end of the third century,[4] the hermits were generally laymen,[5] but were not deprived of the service of priests. Some, like Schenute (333/334-450/451),

---

[1] Canons 107 and 111, § 1.

[2] E.g., canon 964.

[3] Kurtscheid, *Historia Iuris Canonici, Historia Institutorum,* Vol. I, *Ab Ecclesiae Fundatione usque ad Grationum* (Romae: Officium Libri Catholici, 1941), pp. 74-77 (hereafter cited *Historia Institutorum*).

[4] *Ibid.,* p. 177.

[5] Coussa, *Epitome Praelectionum de Iure Ecclesiastico Orientali* (2 vols., Vol. II, Venetiis: Typis Polyglottis Insulae S. Lazari, 1941), II, 19 (hereafter cited *Epitome Iuris Orientalis*).

were priests,[6] who usually had been ordained before they retired into the desert.[7] The number of religious ordained deacons and priests was limited, four or five serving the needs of the monastic church.[8] If it meant leaving their solitude, the early monks themselves seemed loath to receive ordination.[9]

Pope Siricius (384-399) definitely stated that acceptable monks should be raised to the clerical state.[10]

Most monastic rules were silent on the matter of ordination or else treated it but summarily.[11] The Rule of St. Benedict not only allowed clerics to be received into the community,[12] but empowered the abbot to select from among his monks worthy candidates for ordination to the priesthood and diaconate.[13]

Even though popes approved the ordination of religious and regulated the discipline according to which they were ordained, the practice was time and again called into question. The objections, however, centered generally about the exercise of sacerdotal functions among the laity. While these complaints were in a meas-

[6] Kozman, *Textes Legislatifs touchant le Cenobitisme Egyptien,* Codificazione Canonica Orientale, *Fonti,* Series II, Fascicolo I (Civitate Vaticana: Typographie Polyglotte Vaticana, 1935), p. 51.

[7] Kurtscheid, *Historia Institutorum,* p. 177.

[8] Cf. St. Basil, *Epistola 256*—Migne, *Patrologiae Cursus Completus, Series Graeca* (161 vols., Parisiis, 1857-1866), XXXIX, 945 (hereafter cited *PG*); Justinian, N. (132)2.

[9] Cf. St. Athanasius, *Ad Dracontinum*—*PG,* XXV, 531; St. Augustinus, *Ad Eudoxium,* Ep. 48—c. 30, C. XVI, q. 1; Migne, *Patrologiae Cursus Completus, Series Latina* (221 vols., Parisiis, 1844-1864), XXXIII, 188 (hereafter cited *PL*); *Corpus Scriptorum Ecclesiasticorum Latinorum* (Vindobonae, 1866-), XXXIV, ii, 138 (hereafter cited *CSEL*); St. Hieronymus, *Epistola 125*—c. 26, C. XVI, q. 1; *CSEL,* LVI, 136.

[10] "Monachos quoque quos tamen morum gravitas et vitae ac fidei institutio sancta commendat, clericorum officiis aggregari et optamus et volumus."—c. 29, C. XVI, q. 1; *PL,* XIII, 1144; Jaffé, *Regesta Pontificum Romanorum ab condita Ecclesia ad annum post Christum natum MCXCVIII* (2. ed. curaverunt Loewenfeld, Kaltenbrunner, Ewald, 2 vols., Lipsiae, 1885-1888), n. 255 (hereafter cited Jaffé).

[11] Cf. Benedict of Aniane, *Concordia Regularum,* c. LXVII and LXIX—*PL,* CIII, 1313-1316, 1323-1326.

[12] C. LX—Butler, *Sancti Benedicti Regula Monasteriorum* (2. ed., Friburgi Brisgoviae, 1927) (hereafter cited *Regula*).

[13] *Regula,* c. LXII.

ure due to abuses, they did not always rise from the purest of intentions. It should further be remembered that the influence of religious in the ecclesiastical fabric of some countries was based on the parts monks had played in the conversion of Europe to Christianity and civilization.[14]

The monk was reminded that he was a man of penance, not a teacher,[15] and, though ordained, should not abandon his pristine purpose,[16] or usurp functions which belonged to the bishop.[17] Some of the quoted texts,[18] however, were spurious or of an uncertain origin.[19]

Those who defended the ordination and ministry of religious could also cite texts, both spurious[20] and genuine,[21] which allowed monks who were priests to baptize, preach, and minister to souls. The Council of Nimes (1096) considered the ministry of monks more perfect and effective because of their higher station.[22]

Gratian (+ ca. 1157), after considering the conflicting chapters, concluded that monks could licitly exercise sacerdotal functions.[23] Pope Innocent III (1198-1216) likewise justified the ordination of monks, even for parochial work, and based his decision on the practices of the past.[24] The glossators admitted that the

---

[14] Cf. Pius XII, litt. encycl. *"Fulgens radiatur,"* 21 mart. 1947—*Acta Apostolicae Sedis,* XXXIX (1947), 148-149 (hereafter cited *AAS*).

[15] St. Hieronymus, *Ad Riparium et Desiderium*—c. 4, C. XVI, q. 1.

[16] Innocentius I—c. 3, C. XVI, q. 1; Jaffé, n. 286.

[17] Paschalis II, *Victori, Bononiensi Episcopo*—c. 9, C. XVI, q. 1; Jaffé, n. 6616.

[18] C. 1, 8, C. XVI, q. 1.

[19] Cf. *Notationes Correctorum,* Causa XVI, Quest. I, C. 1. Also the comments on these chapters in the *Corpus Iuris Canonici* (ed. Lipsiensis 2. instruxit Friedberg, 2 vols., Lipsiae, 1879-1881).

[20] C. 21, C. XVI, q. 1. Cf. *Notationes Correctorum* on this chapter.

[21] Bonifatius IV—c. 25, C. XVI, q. 1; Jaffé, n. 1996. Cf. Bouix, *Tractatus de Jure Regularium* (2 vols., Parisiis, 1857), II, 5.

[22] Canons 2 and 3—Mansi, *Sacrorum Conciliorum Nova et Amplissima Collectio* (53 vols. in 60, Parisiis, 1901-1927), XX, 931-934 (hereafter cited Mansi).

[23] *Dicta* ad c. 25, C. XVI, q. 1.

[24] C. 5, X, *de statu monachorum et canonicorum regularium,* III, 35; Potthast, *Regesta Pontificium Romanorum inde ab anno post Christum natum MCXCVIII ad annum MCCCIV* (2 vols., Berolini, 1874-1875), n. 1329 (hereafter cited Potthast).

monastic state was not intended for parochial work, but that this practice was allowed by the common law in the form of a general dispensation.[25]

To prevent abuses, Pope Calixtus II (1119-1124) forbade abbots and monks to administer the sacraments publicly. At the same time he restricted the ordination of monks, among other pontifical functions, to the bishop of the diocese in which they lived.[26]

The Canons Regular and the Mendicant orders, which arose in these centuries, provided the Church with a new source of sacerdotal ministers. The attention of legislators and canonists, however, was turned to the new canonical problems which arose with these institutes. Chiefly, the laws and discussions centered about the examination of the ordinand, the selection of the ordaining prelate, and faculties for preaching and absolving.

One more act of legislation was to place the rectitude of ordaining religious beyond question. In the reform program of Pope Clement V (1305-1314), as carried out through the Council of Vienne (1311-1312), monastic life was to take a simpler and stricter character. To increase the worship of God, all monks were to present themselves for ordination at the behest of their abbots.[27]

In more modern times, the synod of Pistoia (1786) proposed a reform of Regulars by defining the incompatibility of the religious and clerical life, by limiting the number of priests in a monastery to one or two, and by restricting the celebration of Holy Mass in monasteries to once or twice a day. Religious, even though ordained, were to refrain from an exercise of their sacerdotal powers; the majority was never to be promoted to orders. These propositions were among the 85 condemned by Pope Pius VI (1775-1799).[28]

---

[25] *Glossa ordinaria* ad v. *regimen in presbyteros,* c. 5, X, *de statu monachorum et canonicorum regularium,* III, 35.

[26] Canon 17, I Council of Lateran (1123)—c. 10, C. XVI, q. 1; Mansi, XXI, 285.

[27] C. 1, *de statu monachorum vel canonicorum regularium,* III, 10, in Clem.

[28] Const. *"Auctorem fidei,"* 28 aug. 1794, nn. 84-85—Denzinger, Bonnwart, Umberg, *Enchiridion Symbolorum, Definitionum, et Declarationum de Rebus Fidei et Morum* (21.-23. ed., Friburgi Brisgoviae: Herder, 1937), nn. 1580, 1585, 1591.

B. THE SCOPE OF THE DISSERTATION

The aim of this work is to present, explain, and co-ordinate the canon law of the Latin Church on the ordination of exempt religious. To this end, the matter is treated with particular attention to the relationships which arise between the candidate, the superior, and the minister. Preference is therefore given to the problems which can and do arise, rather than to a discussion of matters common to all ordinations.

Since the present discipline is based on historical precedents, the contributing factors are treated at those points in the dissertation which seem most appropriate. However, these facts of history have been limited to those which are relevant to the present common law. Individual privileges and exceptions, especially those obtained by the Regulars, have not been treated except in so far as they are now part and parcel of the legislation in the present case.

As this is primarily a study of the discipline affecting sacred ordination, attention is given to the theological basis of the questions treated only to the extent that the Code incorporates theology into the law. Likewise a consideration of the harmony of the priesthood with the specific aims of a particular religious institute, as well as a justification of the exercise of the ministry among the faithful by religious, is perforce entirely omitted.

The matter can be best treated by means of an initial consideration of the qualifications of the candidate, of the problems which arise in admitting him into the institute, of the factors connected with his education and preparation for ordination and his actual promotion to orders, and of the co-ordination of his advance in the religious state with the reception of minor and major orders. The position of the superior should next be considered, his rôle in the ordination described, and his rights and powers determined. The selection of the proper minister for the ordination should then receive attention. Finally, the delicts and penalties which can intervene in the ordination of exempt religious should be enumerated with a view to showing what sanctions the church employs in the upholding of its laws.

Discussion is limited to the law governing the ordination of exempt religious, since the non-exempt religious observe the norm provided for seculars.[29] In the earlier law, the discipline affecting exempt religious was referred to as that of the Regulars. The Code has adopted the term exempt religious, which includes not only Regulars, but also other institutes which enjoy the required degree of exemption from the local ordinary. Hence the term exempt religious should be understood as including Regulars, who are members of religious orders,[30] religious of simple vows who belong to an institute exempt by papal privilege,[31] and members of non-exempt institutes which by privilege or indult are permitted to follow the discipline of exempt religious for the ordination of their members.[32] The applicability of this discipline to the latter class can be correctly determined from the general law only in so far as the grant concedes the various faculties. The most characteristic feature is that the religious are ordained with dimissorial letters from their religious superior, not from the local ordinary.[33]

For the sake of uniformity and brevity, the term *institute* will be used to designate the orders, congregations, and societies which observe this discipline in the ordination of their members. A distinction will sometimes be made, however, when the law provides for exceptions in respect to Regulars or exempt congregations. Since the major superior in a clerical exempt institute is given certain powers as an ordinary,[34] the same faculties are not always applicable to other superiors who may be accorded by privilege or indult the right to prepare dimissorial letters. Such a distinction does not, however, preclude the existence of similar faculties in virtue of a particular grant.

The expressions *major orders* and *sacred orders* are used to designate the priesthood, diaconate, and subdiaconate; the orders

---

[29] Canon 964, 4°.

[30] Canon 615. Cf. canon 488, 2° and 7°.

[31] Canon 618, § 1.

[32] Voltas, "De Domicilio quoad Ordinationem Religiosorum,"—*Commentarium pro Religiosis* (Romae, 1920-1934; ab anno 1935 *Commentarium pro Religiosis et Missionariis*), II (1921), 301 (hereafter cited *CpR, CpRM*).

[33] Cf. canon 964, 2°.

[34] Canon 198.

through which a cleric becomes an acolyte, an exorcist, a lector, or a porter are referred to as *minor orders.*[85] The words *ordination, sacred ordination, order,* and *to ordain* relate not only to the three major and four minor orders, but also to clerical tonsure.[86]

Although some references will be made to Orientals, no effort will be made to undertake a detailed discussion of the legislation specifically applicable to other than the Latin rite. In general, candidates of an Oriental rite are not bound by the discipline under discussion in this dissertation, except in so far as their membership in a Latin rite community places them under the jurisdiction of a superior who is bound to observe these norms in the ordination of his subjects. Since all persons are bound by the prescriptions of their own rite in the reception of the sacraments, Orientals should observe the laws of their own rite as to the age for the reception of orders, the irregularities and impediments, interstices between orders, and the times of the year prescribed for the conferring of orders. On the other hand, by their membership in a Latin rite institute, they are governed by the laws of that community in their relations as religious. Thus the prohibitions against the ordination of novices and against the promotion of religious in temporary vows to major orders are applicable to them.

By Orientals are meant those who retain their rite and discipline even as members of a Latin institute, not such as have obtained from competent ecclesiastical authority a transfer to the Latin rite[87] or at least permission to conform to the Latin discipline.

---

[85] Canon 949.

[86] Canon 950.

[87] Canon 98, § 3.

CHAPTER II

THE CANDIDATE

The ordination of religious in exempt institutes is closely bound up with their religious life. Their affiliation with a particular religious institute is similar to incardination in a diocese.[1] Much of the jursdiction exercised by a bishop over his secular subjects is vested in the religious superior in respect to his religious. While the requirements for ordination of religious candidates are basically the same as for other ordinands, the manner in which these requisites are satisfied involves some modifications because of the membership in the religious institute. Hence it is necessary to treat briefly the requirements of canon law for ordination in so far as they are affected by the fact that the candidate is an exempt religious.

ARTICLE I. PRE-NOVITIATE TRAINING

The preparation of a youth for ordination should begin in the years which precede his acceptance into the religious institute as a novice. The aspirant is to be selected, with due consideration and prudence, for his aptitude for a clerical and religious vocation.[2] The choice should be based on an investigation of the disposition, character, and moral qualities of the individual, with careful consideration given to the purpose, spirit, and reasons which have moved the youth to cherish the religious life.[3] The precise manner in which this preliminary examination is to be made becomes determinable through the regulations and customs of each institute. Although this selection anticipates a more thor-

---

[1] Cf. canon 111; Voltas, "De Domicilio quoad Ordinationem Religiosorum," —*CpR*, II (1921), 302.

[2] S. C. de Religiosis, instr. *"Quantum religiones,"* 1 dec. 1931, n. 5-6—*AAS*, XXIV (1932), 75-76.

[3] Pius IX, ep. *"Ubi primum,"* 17 iun. 1847, as quoted in S. C. de Religiosis, instr. *"Quantum religiones,"* 1 dec. 1931, n. 4—*AAS*, XXIV (1932), 75.

ough investigation which should precede admittance into the novitiate, it is of value in revealing the possible existence of a vocation in the applicants and in eliminating candidates of an undesirable character. Ordinarily this selection is made as a part of the entrance formalities for admittance into the preparatory seminary or school conducted by the institute.

Those candidates who show promise are to receive a suitable training in the lower academic studies. Such a preliminary education under the care and direction of religious is traditional in most institutes, which either conduct a school exclusively set up for candidates, or send them to an educational establishment under their control.[4] Although the Code does not specify the obligation of the religious institute to provide the education in preparatory subjects, Pope Pius XI (1921-1939) removed any doubt in this regard by applying to religious the provisions of canon 1364 on minor seminaries.[5]

These preparatory studies, which are referred to as the "humanities," form the stage of secondary education midway between that of the elementary school and that given in professional schools. In the United States, the elementary (grammar) school course of eight years is usually required as a prerequisite for a youth who is to be admitted to a minor seminary or a high school. This intermediate education comprises that which is given in the four years of high school and the first two years of college.[6] Ordinarily this secondary course is to be completed before the

---

[4] Langasco, *De Institutione Clericorum in Disciplinis Inferioribus* (Romae: Typis Polyglottis Vaticanis, 1936), n. 146. For further discussion on the history, philosophy, and subject of clerical studies among religious, cf. Langasco, *op. cit.*, n. 99-100, 135-146; Bolduc, *Les Études dans les Religions Cléricales*, The Catholic University of America Canon Law Studies, n. 149 (Washington, D. C.: The Catholic University of America Press, 1942), pp. 39-71; Oesterle, "De Ratione Studiorum in Religionibus Clericalibus,"—*CpR*, V (1924), 444-460; VI (1925), 34-42, 141-146, 191-202, 296-323. An older apology is that by Mabillon, *Tractatus de Studiis Monasticis* (3 vols., Venetiis, 1745), Pars I, c. iv.

[5] Ep. ap. *"Unigenitus Dei Filius,"* 19 mart. 1924—*AAS*, XVI (1924), 133. Cf. S. C. de Religiosis, instr. *"Quantum religiones,"* 1 dec. 1931, n. 4-5—*AAS*, XXIV (1932), 75-76.

[6] Beste, *Introductio in Codicem* (3. ed., Collegeville, Minn.: St. John's Abbey Press, 1946), pp. 680-681 (hereafter cited *Introductio*).

candidate enters the novitiate, though for a grave reason the youth may be admitted earlier. In the latter case the "humanities" are to be completed before the study of philosophy is begun.[7] The determination of the gravity of the cause is left to the superior who admits the candidate to the novitiate. Since a candidate who has completed his classical course will usually derive greater benefits from the novitiate than a candidate insufficiently prepared,[8] the motivating reason should be sufficiently serious to warrant the exception to the common norm. Thus, if a candidate would be excused from compulsory military service only if he were enrolled in the major seminary or if he were a professed religious, superiors would seem to be justified in accepting such a candidate before the completion of his secondary studies.[9]

While considerable liberty is allowed in the designing of the curriculum, conformity with the educational programs outlined by recognized authorities in the various regions is desirable.[10] The studies should provide the future cleric with that equipment which is expected of a cultured person. Religion must receive primary attention, and the Latin and vernacular languages especially should be studied.[11]

ARTICLE II. ADMITTANCE INTO THE NOVITIATE

After the candidate has advanced sufficiently in age and studies, his admission into the novitiate[12] can be considered. At this point the candidate is subject to a further investigation in order that

[7] Canon 589, § 1; S. C. de Religiosis, instr. "*Quantum religiones,*" 1 dec. 1931, n. 5—*AAS,* XXIV (1932), 75-76.

[8] Beste, *Introductio,* p. 406.

[9] Thus, under the Selective Training and Service Act of 1940, students who were preparing for the ministry in recognized divinity schools were exempt from service (but not from registration) under the Act. Since the educational level of the school was not specified, the superior could justly accept such students who, though preparing for the priesthood, were not registered in a recognized seminary. Cf. *United States Code* (1940 ed., 4 vols., Washington, D. C.: United States Government Printing Office, 1941), Title 50, § 305 (d).

[10] Coronata, *Institutiones Iuris Canonici* (2. ed., 5 vols., Taurini-Romae: Marietti, 1939-1947), II, n. 941, 1, c (hereafter cited *Institutiones*).

[11] Cf. canon 1364.

[12] Unless the particular institute has a contrary requirement, the postulancy is not required for novices aspiring to the clerical state. Cf. canon 539, § 1.

there may be determined more precisely the presence of the qualities required for the religious life and the clerical state. It is difficult to be too careful in making the selection of candidates, since the youth, once he has been admitted to the religious life, will normally use every effort to remain, even though he is found wanting. Further, the elimination of candidates who do not show promise is an act of mercy to the applicant, of justice to the Church. If allowed to continue, only to be eliminated later, the student returns to the world advanced in years, lettered in a science of little material advantage, and frequently branded by public opinion as a failure.[13] It should be the concern of priests to encourage youths who give indication of a sacerdotal vocation;[14] but it is wrong to force a candidate to embrace the clerical state or the religious life.[15] While God will not permit the Church to suffer from a lack of priests,[16] canonically suitable candidates may not be arbitrarily excluded.[17]

It is important, moreover, that the character and dispositions of the applicant be examined at this time with a view to his religious and clerical vocation. Since his state will differ from that of a lay religious, and since he will be subject to obligations which are not imposed on the secular clergy, the superiors have the duty to ascertain the candidate's aptitude for the religious-clerical life as it is lived in the particular institute.[18]

The examination of the qualities of the aspirant to the novitiate is designed as a means for revealing the presence of those qualities which experience and prudence deem necessary for a successful vocation, as also the absence of defects considered harmful. In addition to the details gathered from the observation of the student at the preparatory school, the testimonial letters furnish informa-

---

[13] Cf. S. C. de Sacramentis, instr. *"Quam ingens,"* 27 dec. 1930, § 1, n. 3—*AAS,* XXIII (1931), 121.

[14] Canon 1353.

[15] Canons 971, 2352.

[16] Pius XI, litt. encycl. *"Ad catholici sacerdotii,"* 25 dec. 1935—*AAS,* XXVIII (1936), 44.

[17] Canon 971.

[18] Canon 538; S. C. de Religiosis, instr. *"Quantum religiones,"* 1 dec. 1931, n. 6—*AAS,* XXIV (1932), 76.

tion which may not be otherwise available to the superior.[19] The moral qualities of the candidate's family should also be investigated with a view to discovering the possible existence of undesirable traits which might reappear in the aspirant.[20]

It is not sufficient, however, to consider the qualities of the candidate for the priesthood in a general manner, for the legislator has placed freedom from irregularities and canonical impediments as a condition for the licit admission to the novitiate of a candidate destined for the priesthood.[21] Bishops are alerted not to admit candidates of illegitimate birth into the seminary,[22] and to give due consideration to the debarring effects of the other irregularities and impediments.[23]

Since, in a way, entrance into the novitiate is similar to enrollment in a seminary, the Code prohibits the admission of candidates for the priesthood if they are debarred from the clerical state because of an irregularity or impediment. This prohibition, which affects the licitness of admission to the novitiate, does not directly make the irregularity or impediment a hindrance for entering the novitiate as such, but rather considers the debarment from the reception of orders as disqualifying the candidate from the particular novitiate in question. A candidate for the lay-brotherhood is unaffected by the prohibition, even though he would be irregular for the priesthood.[24]

The terms *irregularity* and *canonical impediment* are technical expressions with a restricted meaning in the present law. The irregularities are completely[25] enumerated in canons 984 and 985.

---

[19] Canon 544-545.

[20] S. C. de Religiosis, instr. "*Quantum religiones,*" 1 dec. 1931, n. 6—*AAS*, XXIV (1932), 76.

[21] Canon 542, 2°: Illicite, sed valide admittuntur . . . ad sacerdotium in religione destinati, a quo tamen removeantur irregularitate aliove canonico impedimento.

[22] Canon 1363, § 1.

[23] S. C. de Sacramentis, instr. "*Quam ingens,*" 27 dec. 1930, § 1, n. 2—*AAS*, XXIII (1931), 121.

[24] If, by special arrangement, all the novices make the same novitiate, and only at the time of profession are selected for the clerical or lay state, this provision of canon 542 does not apply. Cf. Larraona, "Commentarium Codicis" —*CpRM*, XVIII (1937), 149.

[25] Canon 983.

While some question may be raised as to the extent of the term *canonical impediment,* it should be noted that the heading *De irregularitatibus aliisque impedimentis* is used for the article which embraces canons 983 to 991, while the other requisites such as the attainment of a given age, the completion of the theological studies, and the possession of a canonical title are described under the heading *De requisitis in subiecto sacrae ordinationis.*[26] It seems proper, therefore, to understand the impediments to ordination as those which are listed in canon 987. Moreover, the prohibition of canon 542, 2°, limits the liberty of a candidate to enter a religious institute,[27] so that a strict interpretation of the restrictions seems in order.[28] It appears proper, then, to include under the enacted prohibition of canon 542, 2°, only those irregularities and impediments which are described in canons 984, 985, and 987.[29]

Although the prohibition against admitting into the novitiate those candidates who are destined for the priesthood but debarred from orders because of an irregularity or impediment is an innovation introduced by the Code, the law is not without some historical foundation. While monks and Canons Regular were not bound by the irregularity arising from illegitimate birth,[30] Pope Sixtus V (1585-1590) prohibited, under threat of invalidity, the reception into monasteries of candidates of illegitimate birth, as well as those who were under threat of condemnation for a public crime.[31] These crimes were of such a nature as to give rise to an irregularity arising from a delict.

---

[26] While these requisites are necessary for a licit ordination (canon 974, § 1), in pre-Code law they were sometimes included among the impediments. Cf. Gasparri, *Tractatus Canonicus de Sacra Ordinatione* (2 vols., Parisiis, 1893-1894), n. 120, 139, 477-614 (hereafter cited *De Sacra Ordinatione*).

[27] Cf. canon 538.

[28] Canon 19.

[29] Cf. Blat, *Commentarium Textus Codicis Iuris Canonici* (5 vols. in 7, Romae, 1921-1927), II, n. 610, 2°.

[30] Council of Poitiers (1078), canon 8—Mansi, XX, 498-499; c. 1, X, *de filiis presbyterorum ordinandis vel non,* I, 17.

[31] Const. *"Cum de omnibus,"* 26 nov. 1587, § 1-4—*Codicis Iuris Canonici Fontes cura Emi Petri Card. Gasparri editi* (9 vols., Romae [postea Civitate Vaticana]: Typis Polyglottis Vaticanis, 1923-1939; [Vols. VII-IX ed. cura et studio Emi Iustiniani Card. Serédi]), n. 162 (hereafter cited *Fontes*); const. *"Ad Romanum,"* 21 oct. 1588, § 4, 17—*Fontes,* n. 164.

Because of abuses occasioned by the legislation of Pope Sixtus V, for some religious abandoned the religious life on the plea that they were not validly professed, Pope Gregory XIV (1590-1591)[82] and Pope Clement VIII (1592-1605) abrogated that discipline.[83] These prohibitions against the reception of candidates of illegitimate birth or of such as were guilty of crime were established for the purpose of preserving the dignity of the religious life; yet, in so far as an irregularity was also present, the clerical state was indirectly protected. Although some religious institutes required candidates to be free from irregularities and impediments to orders, this was not demanded by the common law.[84]

The text of canon 542, 2°, seems quite clear, and if it be interpreted in its context it reveals the prohibition to be the following: A candidate for the priesthood in a religious institute, if he is under an irregularity or impediment which debars him from ordination, may not be licitly received into the novitiate. The purpose, moreover, is quite evident. If a candidate who is debarred from orders be admitted to the novitiate and thereafter allowed to continue his preparation for the priesthood, either he must be refused orders because of the canonical defect, or a dispensation must be obtained under conditions which leave but little to the judgment of the grantor. To forestall the occasion of such a *casus perplexus,* the prohibition against admitting into the novitiate a candidate debarred from the priesthood was introduced into the Code.[85]

The law of canon 542, 2°, taken in its literal sense, requires freedom from irregularities and impediments before the aspirant is admitted to the novitiate. Not only does the text make no exception for those irregularities and impediments which, before the candidate is ready for orders, will cease to disqualify the

---

[82] Const. "*Circumspecta,*" 15 mart. 1591, § 2—*Fontes,* n. 170.

[83] Const. "*In suprema,*" 2 apr. 1602, § 3—*Bullarum Diplomatum et Privilegiorum Sanctorum Pontificum Taurinensis Editio* (24 vols. et Appendix, Augustae Taurinorum, 1857-1872), X, 768-769 (hereafter cited *Bull. Rom. Taur.*).

[84] Cf. S. C. S. Off., 3 febr. 1898, ad 1—*Fontes,* n. 1196.

[85] Oesterle, "De Potestate Superiorum Maiorum in Religionibus Clericalibus Exemptis"—*CpRM,* XXV (1944-1946), 39-47.

ordinand, but the very listing of this provision as a requisite for the novitiate implies that the legislator desires to have the matter decided before the religious life is begun. The only conclusion which seems warranted is that the irregularity or impediment must have either ceased or been dispensed before the candidate is admitted to the novitiate.[36]

Canonists, however, admit a variety of exceptions. These can be grouped into schools of thought which become successively more generous in the exceptions allowed. Of the authors consulted, none requires that a candidate who is irregular in consequence of his illegitimacy needs to obtain a dispensation before the novitiate if solemn vows will be made before ordination.[37] For the profession of solemn vows removes the irregularity arising from illegitimacy without further intervention of any authority. Before this solemn profession, however, a Regular could not be licitly promoted even to tonsure and minor orders unless the irregularity first ceased or was dispensed.

A more liberal group adds to this exception those irregularities and impediments which, without the intervention of the Holy See, will certainly cease to bind before ordination, either through the factual cessation of the cause itself or through a remission of the disqualification effected with faculties communicated by the law or by privilege.[38] The conditions expressed effectively limit the irregularities and impediments which can be expected. The first

---

[36] Oesterle, *loc. cit.;* Toso, *Ad Codicem Iuris Canonici Commentaria Minora* (5 vols., Romae, 1920-1927), II, ii, 99; Blat, *loc. cit.;* Sipos, *Enchiridion Iuris Canonici* (4. ed., Pécs: Ex Typographia "Haladás R. T.," 1940), § 68, I, 2.

[37] Cf. canon 984, 1°. Toso (*loc. cit.*) proposes this exception with some anxiety. Prümmer requires a dispensation to be sought before the admission to the novitiate of those future Regulars who will be ordained before their solemn profession. Cf. *Manuale Iuris Canonici* (6. ed., Friburgi Brisgoviae: Herder, 1933), Q. 205, 5, footnote 11.

[38] Voltas, "Consultationes"—*CpR,* II (1921), 369; Vermeersch-Creusen, *Epitome Iuris Canonici* (6. ed., 3 vols., Mechlinae-Romae: Dessain, 1937-1946), I, n. 686 (hereafter cited *Epitome*); Beste, *Introductio,* p. 367; Schaefer, *De Religiosis Ad Normam Codicis Iuris Canonici* (4. ed., Romae: Editrice "Apostolico Cattolico," 1947), n. 221, 5 (hereafter cited *De Religiosis*); Larraona, "Commentarium Codicis"—*CpRM,* XVIII (1937), 150.

condition is that the disqualifying effect is of such a nature that it will certainly cease before the time of ordination; if only the possibility of cessation is present, then a dispensation is to be sought before the candidate is admitted to the novitiate. The second condition is that the means whereby the remission is to be effected be already within the power of the candidate or of another, usually the superior. For, when the candidate enters the religious community, both he and the superior implicitly agree to do all that is necessary for the eventual ordination of the candidate.

Especially important in this respect are the faculties of major superiors in exempt clerical communities, in their position as ordinaries, to dispense their subjects from irregularities arising from occult delicts, except those of homicide, abortion, and such as have been brought to the judicial forum,[39] and to determine when the impediments arising from recent conversion and from infamy of fact have ceased.[40] Since the religious superior is ordinarily not the candidate's ordinary before the novitiate is begun, he cannot use these faculties on behalf of the aspirant at that time. Yet, because both the capacity to act and the intention to remit the disqualification are present, the remission of the irregularity or impediment is little short of certain.

While the prohibition of canon 542, 2°, taken literally and by itself does not allow for any exceptions, still, there would be little point to the provision of canon 984, 1°, regarding the effect of solemn profession on illegitimacy, if a dispensation had to be sought before the novitiate. Oesterle, who presents the most cogent case in defense of a literal interpretation of canon 542, 2°, himself admits but does not justify the exception of canon 984, 1°.[41] Yet, if the provision of canon 984, 1°, is allowed as an exception, there is no basis for rejecting other exceptions which are based on other faculties contained in the law, as in canons 990, § 1, and 987, 6°-7°. It therefore seems safely within the spirit of the law to maintain the opinion which excepts from the letter of canon 542, 2°, those irregularities and impediments which, though pres-

---

[39] Canon 990, § 1.

[40] Canon 987, 6°-7°.

[41] *Loc. cit.*

ent at the time of admission to the novitiate, will certainly have ceased to debar the candidate by the time of ordination, either inasmuch as the cause of the irregularity or the impediment will have ended, or inasmuch as a remission will have been granted through faculties communicated by law or privilege.

A third group of authors is still more generous in that it allows admission to the novitiate without previous dispensation also to such candidates as are under an irregularity or impediment which is readily dispensed by the Holy See, and from which a dispensation will be sought in due time.[42] The chief objection to this opinion seems to be the presumption on the part of the religious superior and the candidate that in the particular instance a dispensation will be granted. Since a dispensation is an act of grace and is in no way due to the petitioner, the grantor, even though he may ordinarily grant the favor, is under no obligation to do so in every case. The procedure seems to pre-judge the case, and this by the recipient of the dispensation.[43] These considerations make this last opinion difficult to justify with the spirit, and much less the letter, of the law. Moreover the situation resolves itself essentially to the discipline before the Code, and for practical purposes almost abrogates the salutary provisions introduced in the present law. Despite the great extrinsic authority of the proponents of this opinion, one hesitates to urge the practice.

While one of the requisites for licit admission to the novitiate is freedom from irregularities and impediments to orders, the latter have counterparts in some of the other requirements for entrance into religion. Although this dissertation does not propose to discuss individually the several irregularities and impediments to orders,[44] or the various requisites for admission to the novi-

---

[42] Coronata, *Institutiones*, I, n. 571, 5°; Cappello, *Summa Iuris Canonici* (3 vols., Vols. I-II, 4. ed., 1945; Vol. III, 2. ed., 1940, Romae: Apud Aedes Universitatis Gregorianae), II, n. 37, 5°; Fanfani, *De Iure Religiosorum ad Normam Codicis Iuris Canonici* (2. ed., Taurini-Romae, 1925), n. 180.

[43] Oesterle, *loc. cit.*; Vermeersch-Creusen, *loc. cit.*; Beste, *loc. cit.*

[44] For such information, cf. Hickey, *Irregularities and Simple Impediments in the New Code of Canon Law,* The Catholic University of American Canon Law Studies, n. 7 (Washington, D. C.: The Catholic University of America, 1920); Vogelpohl, *The Simple Impediments to Holy Orders,* The Catholic

tiate,[45] it seems of value to indicate the correlation which is found between them.

A candidate who has belonged to a non-Catholic sect[46] can also be under the irregularity arising from apostasy, heresy, or schism,[47] and the irregularity arising from infamy of law[48] incurred because of the delict against the faith.[49] Although converts from heresy or schism who have never belonged to the Church are not included among those prohibited from entering religious institutes,[50] the practice of the Holy See is to consider those as non-Catholics who, though born of heretical parents, have in adult age received baptism, and thus likewise are affected with the irregularity which arises from the factor of a lack of the faith.[51] The convert may also be subject to the irregularity arising from the reception of baptism from a non-Catholic minister,[52] and to the impediment occasioned by the fact that his parents were not Catholics, unless in the meantime they have become converted or have died.[53] If the candidate has only recently been converted, his status as a neophyte also is an impediment to orders.[54]

A married man, as long as the matrimonial bond continues, is forbidden admission to the novitiate[55] and is impeded from the

---

University of America Canon Law Studies, n. 224 (Washington, D. C.: The Catholic University of America Press, 1945); Coronata, *De Sacramentis Tractatus Canonicus* (3 vols., Taurini-Romae: Marietti, 1943-1946), II, n. 96-169 (hereafter cited *De Sacramentis*); Cappello, *Tractatus Canonico-Moralis de Sacramentis*, Vol. IV (2. ed., Taurini-Romae: Marietti, 1947), nn. 435-529 (hereafter cited *De Sacra Ordinatione*).

[45] For such information, cf. Coronata, *Institutiones*, I, n. 570-572; Schaefer, *De Religiosis*, n. 220-221.

[46] Canon 542, 1°.

[47] Canon 985, 1°.

[48] Canon 984, 5°.

[49] Canon 2314, § 1, 2°-3°.

[50] P.C.I., 16 oct. 1919, ad 7—*AAS*, XI (1919), 477.

[51] Sartori, *Jurisprudentiae Ecclesiasticae Elementa* (Romae: Pontif. Athenaeum Antonianum, 1946), p. 33 (hereafter cited *Jurisprudentia*).

[52] Canon 985, 2°.

[53] Canon 987, 1°.

[54] Canon 987, 6°.

[55] Canon 542, 1°.

reception of orders.[56] If the candidate has married a second time, the irregularity arising from bigamy is also present.[57] Had marriage been attempted while one of the parties was bound by the bond of another marriage, of holy orders, or of religious profession, the aspirant may be irregular because of the delict.[58]

Those who are under threat of a penalty because of a serious crime of which they have been or can be accused cannot be validly admitted into the novitiate,[59] and, depending on the nature of the crime, may also be under an irregularity arising from the criminal act in its nature of a delict,[60] or arising from infamy of law[61] if the crime is thus punished.[62] Such applicants may also be impeded from the reception of orders because of infamy of fact.[63]

Candidates who are under obligation to render an account or are otherwise involved with secular affairs, from which litigation or annoyance may result for the religious institute, may not be licitly admitted to the novitiate,[64] and may also be impeded from the reception of orders if the office or administration is such as is forbidden to clerics.[65]

The irregularities arising from physical or spiritual defects[66] may be of such a nature as to make the candidate unable to bear the burdens of the religious life.[67] An applicant with such defects should rather be advised to seek a community in which he could be a useful member.

If the religious superior prefers to understand the requisite of freedom from irregularities and impediments in the strict and literal sense, it will always be necessary to obtain the dispensation from the irregularity or impediment to orders before the candi-

---

[56] Canon 987, 2°.

[57] Canon 984, 4°.

[58] Canon 985, 3°.

[59] Canon 542, 1°.

[60] Canon 985.

[61] Canon 984, 5°.

[62] Cf. canons 2314, § 1, 2°-3°; 2320; 2328; 2343, § 1, 2° and § 2, 2°; 2351, § 2; 2356; 2357, § 1; 2359, § 2.

[63] Canon 987, 7°. Cf. canon 2293, § 3.

[64] Canon 542, 2°.

[65] Canon 987, 3°.

[66] Canon 984, 2°-3°.

[67] Canon 538.

date is admitted to the novitiate. Even when the more liberal explanation is accepted, a dispensation before the novitiate will still be necessary in those cases in which the irregularity or the impediment will not certainly cease before the candidate is to be ordained, and also in thoses cases in which the condition which gives rise to the irregularity or the impediment likewise prohibits admission into the novitiate.

When the cause which gives rise to the irregularity or the impediment ceases, the disqualifying effect also terminates. Not all of the irregularities and impediments can end in this way, but only those which are based on a condition that can be changed. All the simple impediments[68] and also those irregularities which arise from illegitimacy, physical defects, and infamy of law[69] are of such a nature that it is possible for them to cease by the termination of the cause from which they arise. The other irregularities, which arise from a former act or previous state, obviously cannot end in this manner, since their basis is beyond recall. The disqualifying effect of all irregularities and impediments, even of those which can cease intrinsically, may also cease through dispensation, though at present the favor is not granted for all irregularities and impediments.[70]

The Roman Pontiff, though he personally dispenses at times, regularly operates through the Sacred Congregations. The Sacred Congregation of Religious is competent to dispense from irregularities and impediments to orders when the candidate aspires to the priesthood in the religious life.[71] A candidate of an Oriental rite, even though a religious, approaches the Sacred Congregation for the Oriental Church.[72] Whenever a dispensation is required

[68] Canon 987.

[69] Canon 984, 1°, 2°, 5°.

[70] Cappello, *De Sacra Ordinatione*, nn. 512, 514, 526-529; Coronata, *De Sacramentis*, II, nn. 162-163; Vogelpohl, *The Simple Impediments to Holy Orders*, pp. 54, 87, 104, 164.

[71] Coetus peculiaris S. R. E. Cardinalium, 24 mart. 1919, ad III—*AAS*, XI (1919), 251.

[72] Canon 257, § 2. Cf. Beste, *Introductio*, p. 543; Diederichs, *The Jurisdiction of the Latin Ordinaries over their Oriental Subjects*, The Catholic University of America Canon Law Studies, n. 229 (Washington, D. C.: The Catholic University of America Press, 1946), p. 104.

from an irregularity or an impediment which arises from the lack of the faith, the practice is to direct the petition to the Sacred Congregation of the Holy Office, even when religious or Oriental rite candidates are involved.[73]

The Sacred Penitentiary is competent to dispense in cases which involve the internal forum exclusively,[74] even for candidates of the Oriental rite.[75]

Ordinaries, either personally or through another, can dispense their subjects from irregularities arising from an occult delict, unless the crime be that of an effectively procured abortion, of voluntary homicide, or one that has been brought to the judicial forum.[76] This power is granted to all ordinaries, and therefore is a faculty also of major superiors in clerical exempt religious institutes.[77] Since a candidate for the novitiate is not yet the subject of the religious superior, the ordinary competent to dispense is the bishop of the candidate's domicile.[78] When a neophyte has proved himself sufficiently stable in the faith, and when infamy of fact is no longer present, the impediments arising from these conditions cease. The judgment of the ordinary, however, is to determine when this cessation has supervened.[79] This decision of the ordinary is not a dispensation, but an authoritative declaration that the basis of the impediment no longer exists.

While the faculties granted to ordinaries are limited, they can dispense when the fact of the irregularity or of the impediment is doubtful, provided that the Roman Pontiff is wont to dispense in such cases.[80] When there is danger of grave harm, and the irregularity or the impediment is one from which the Holy See dispenses, the ordinary, for a just and reasonable cause, can use his extraordinary power to dispense if recourse to the Holy See

---

[73] Sartori, *Jurisprudentia*, p. 33.

[74] Canon 258, § 1.

[75] S. C. pro Eccl. Or., resp. 26 iul. 1930—*AAS*, XXII (1930), 394.

[76] Canon 990, § 1.

[77] Canon 198, § 1.

[78] Cf. Coronata, *De Sacramentis*, II, n. 164; Gasparri, *De Sacra Ordinatione*, n. 217-219.

[79] Canon 987, 6°-7°.

[80] Canon 15.

is difficult[81] even through the Apostolic Delegate for the territory.[82]

Since the Code has not revoked any of the faculties or privileges which are of a more generous nature in this matter, religious superiors, especially Regulars, can retain the more extensive grants of the past. The precise extent of these privileges will depend on the tenor of the concession.[83]

When the Holy See is petitioned for a dispensation both for admission to the novitiate and for the remission of an irregularity or impediment to orders, permission may be granted by the Holy See to allow the candidate to be accepted into the institute, though at the same time there be not granted any dispensation from the irregularity or impediment to orders. Recourse will then be necessary before ordination.[84] This seems to be the practice of the Sacred Congregation of the Holy Office in dispensing in cases which involve the factor of a lack of the faith in its nature of an irregularity.[85] In this way the assertions and statements of the initial petition are verified by evidence of the candidate's stability.[86] The distinction which is drawn between the dispensation required, on the one hand, for licit admission to the novitiate and, on the other hand, for promotion to orders finds a parallel in the admission of a candidate of illegitimate birth into the diocesan seminary. Although a youth born outside of wedlock should not

---

[81] Canons 81; 84, § 1.

[82] P. C. I., 26 iun. 1947, ad B, I—*AAS*, XXXIX (1947), 373-374.

[83] Cf. Shuhler, *Privileges of Regulars to Absolve and Dispense*, The Catholic University of America Canon Law Studies, n. 186 (Washington, D. C.: The Catholic University of America Press, 1943), pp. 158-159, 163, 170; Capobianco, *Privilegia et Facultates Ordinis Fratrum Minorum* (Salerno: Ex Conventu S. M. Angelorum, 1946), n. 133-149.

[84] Blat, *Commentarium Textus Codicis Iuris Canonici*, II, n. 610, 2°; Vermeersch, "Canon 542, 2°, et Dispensatio ab Irregularitate"—*Periodica de Religiosis et Missionariis* (Brugis, 1905-1919; *Periodica de Re Canonica et Morali utili praesertim Religiosis et Missionariis*, 1920-1927; *Periodica de Re Canonica, Morali, Liturgica*, 1927—), XX (1931), 136*-137* (hereafter cited *Periodica*).

[85] Sartori, *Jurisprudentia*, p. 33.

[86] Cf. Procura Generalis O. F. M., monitum—*Acta Ordinis Fratrum Minorum* (Ad Claras Aquas, 1882—), LIX (1940), 233-234 (hereafter cited *Acta Minorum*).

be admitted to the seminary,[87] the Apostolic Delegates normally enjoy the faculty to permit this, apart, however, from remitting the irregularity.[88]

The requirement that the candidate for the novitiate be free of irregularities and impediments relates to the licit, and not to the valid, admission to the novitiate.[89] If the presence of an irregularity or impediment is discovered after the novitiate has been begun, the candidate is allowed to continue, and a dispensation is to be sought before ordination.[90] But there exists a sufficient reason for his dismissal if the presence of the irregularity or the impediment had been maliciously concealed, or if the Holy See is not wont to dispense from the irregularity or impediment.[91]

If the candidate for the novitiate belongs to an Oriental rite, the written permission of the Sacred Congregation for the Oriental Church is required for his licit admission to the novitiate.[92] Because of the inconvenience which would arise in a religious community in which one or the other member observed another rite, entrance into a Latin rite institute would amount to a transfer of rite. Since such a change may not be made on private authority, the Holy See reserves to itself the granting of the necessary permission.[93]

The Sacred Congregation for the Propagation of the Faith, to whose care the Oriental Church was then entrusted, required recourse to the Holy See when an Oriental rite candidate wished to enter a Latin rite institute, and there to be promoted to orders.[94] The petition was to state the name, the age, the rite, and the diocese of the candidate, the nature of the institute he wished to

---

[87] Canon 1363, § 1.

[88] Cf. "Additional Faculties, c"—Bouscaren, *The Canon Law Digest* (2 vols., Milwaukee: Bruce, 1934-1943), II, 186.

[89] Canon 542, 2°.

[90] Schaefer, *De Religiosis*, n. 221, 5°; Vermeersch-Creusen, *Epitome*, I, n. 688.

[91] Coronata, *Institutiones*, I, n. 571, 7°; Beste, *Introductio*, p. 368.

[92] Canon 542, 2°.

[93] Creusen, "Admission d'Orientaux au Noviciat"—*Revue des Communautés Religieuses* (Louvain, 1925-), II (1926), 41.

[94] 1 iun. 1885, ad 1, b—*Fontes*, n. 4909.

join, and his intention to enter the clerical state, unless he preferred to remain a lay religious.[95] Since the present practice retains the discipline of the past, the petition containing these details is sent, together with a testimonial from the candidate's ordinary,[96] to the Sacred Congregation for the Oriental Church.[97]

The candidate is allowed to enter the novitiate; but, before he makes profession, recourse is again to be invoked for a definitive transfer which will be effected by his pronouncing of vows and will permit him to observe the Latin rite discipline also for promotion to orders. The grant generally contains the provision that, should the candidate leave the institute for any cause whatsoever, he is bound to follow his former rite, and is forbidden both to exercise the orders already received and to be promoted to higher orders without the permission of the Holy See.[98]

No permission of the Holy See is required, however, if candidates of an Oriental rite are accepted into a religious institute in order to establish religious houses of that Oriental rite.[99] Thus Pope Pius XI (1922-1939) desired that one Benedictine monastery in each country be engaged in preparing monks of the Byzantine-Slavonic rite for missionary work among the dissident Russians.[100] Novices and religious of an Oriental rite do not in this case undergo a change of rite and, even though subject to a superior in a Latin rite institute, are held to the laws of their own rite which are intimately connected with the reception of orders.[101] Such religious therefore are subject to the laws on irregularities, interstices, and age for ordination as provided for in their particular rite.

---

[95] S. C. de Prop. Fide, ep. 15 iun. 1912—*Fontes,* n. 4943; *AAS,* IV (1912), 534-535.

[96] Leo XIII, litt. ap. *"Orientalium,"* 30 nov. 1894, X—*Fontes,* n. 627.

[97] Coussa, *Epitome Iuris Orientalis,* n. 66, g.

[98] Sartori, *Jurisprudentia,* p. 35.

[99] P. C. I., 10 nov. 1925, ad VI—*AAS,* XVII (1925), 583.

[100] Ep. *"Equidem,"* 21 mart. 1924—*Annales Ordinis S. Benedicti* (Sublaci, 1893-), XXVIII-XXXIV (1920-1926), 87-88 (hereafter cited *Annales OSB*).

[101] Diederichs, *The Jurisdiction of the Latin Ordinaries over their Oriental Subjects,* p. 55.

If the candidate for the novitiate had for any reason left a seminary, the superior, before admitting the applicant, must first approach the Sacred Congregation of Religious, which in each case will inform the superior of the proper procedure.[102] This new[103] provision does not constitute another impediment or requisite to admission into the novitiate, but rather prescribes a new procedure, since it requires the religious superior to obtain the decision of the Sacred Congregation before admitting a former seminarian who has been dismissed from a seminary, or who has left it, willingly or otherwise, with the idea of abandoning his ecclesiastical vocation. Not affected by the decree are those seminarians who, after completing their studies, leave to await the time for ordination, who licitly interrupt their studies to pursue some special classes, or who have been compelled to leave because of an obligation, e.g., of military service, but do not meanwhile abandon their vocation.[104] Seminarians who leave the seminary or college in order to embrace the religious life are likewise not comprehended under the decree, since sufficient provision for such changes is made in canon 544, § 3.[105]

In cases wherein recourse must be invoked, the Sacred Congregation of Religious is to be provided with documents and testimonials, signed by the rector of the seminary in which the candidate had studied, describing the moral and intellectual qualities of the applicant, the studies completed together with a transcript of the grades received, the extent of the aspirant's inclination and aptitude for the religious life, the reasons for which he left the seminary, and, especially if he had been dismissed, the manner of

[102] Ss. Cc. de Religiosis atque de Seminariis et Studiorum Universitatibus, decr. 25 iul. 1941—*AAS,* XXXIII (1941), 371.

[103] Before the Code, dismissed seminarians could not be accepted into religious institutes. Cf. S. C. de Religiosis, decr. 7 sept. 1909—*Fontes,* n. 4396.

[104] La Puma, "Adnotationes"—*CpRM,* XXIII (1942), 226-237. This article was summarily reported by Frison, "Ex-Seminarian and Novice: A Clarification"—*The Jurist* (Washington, 1941-), VI (1946), 416-418.

[105] S. C. de Religiosis, dubium, 11 maii 1942—*Acta Minorum,* LXI (1942), 125; *CpRM,* XXIII (1942), 238; Frison, *loc. cit.* This was a private reply given to the Minister General of the Friars Minor and appears identical with that given to the General of the Society of Jesus, as reported by Bouscaren, *The Canon Law Digest,* II, 166.

this departure.[106] On the basis of this information, the Sacred Congregation will determine whether or not the applicant may be admitted to the novitiate.

The other prescriptions of canon law and of the constitutions proper to each institute are, of course, to be observed in the admitting of the applicant into the novitiate. Consideration has been given to only those items which are related to the eventual ordination of the candidate.

ARTICLE III. THE NOVITIATE

The novitiate made by the clerical novice is juridically,[107] physically,[108] and ascetically distinct from that of the *conversi*.[109] The purpose of this period of training is primarily to acquaint the tyro with the nature and obligations of religious life and to initiate him into the acquisition of spiritual perfection.[110] The novitiate is not directly concerned with the clerical state, even though its experiences will ordinarily further the development of qualities desired in any priest.

During the period of the novitiate, the novice is not to engage in the study of letters, of the sciences, or of the arts,[111] but may devote some time to practice in the Latin or vernacular language, to the perusal of the Fathers of the Church, or to exercises in public reading and chant. For such activities are not avowedly carried on with an academic motive, but rather for the maintenance of a wholesome acquaintance with intellectual activity.[112] But it would defeat one of the purposes of the novitiate if the candidate were to complete his academic pre-requisites or antic-

---

[106] Sartori, *Jurisprudentia*, p. 36. Cardinal La Puma (*loc. cit.*) felt that there should also be an indication of the superior's agreement with or dissent from the rector's statements.

[107] Canon 558.

[108] Canon 654, § 2.

[109] Canon 565, § 2-3.

[110] Canon 565, § 1.

[111] Canon 565, § 3.

[112] Cf. S. C. de Religiosis, decr., 27 aug. 1910—*Fontes*, n. 4405; Beste, *Introductio*, pp. 381-382.

ipate the professional curriculum. It does not seem proper, therefore, to evaluate the activities of the novitiate as courses for scholastic credit; for either the studies become a distraction from the real activity of the novitiate, or standards are relaxed to become a mockery of legitimate education.[113] The novitiate can well serve as a transition to the professional work of philosophy and theology and as a point of orientation for the future.

Not only are studies during the novitiate forbidden, but promotion to orders likewise is not allowed.[114] Since in practice the reception of orders is governed by progress in the required classes of the curriculum, the occasion will but seldom arise that a novice is ready for ordination.

The glossators counseled that tonsure should not be conferred during the year of probation.[115] The prohibition forbidding the ordination of novices was incorporated into the decree *Auctis admodum;* but this law forbade only superiors to prepare dimissorials for the promotion of novices to major orders,[116] since this right belonged to the novice's bishop.[117] The prohibition, as it is stated in the Code, forbids the ordination of the novice. The superior is incapable of granting the dimissorial letters, since the candidate is not a professed religious.[118] The bishop too is enjoined from promoting the novice to orders.[119] Should it become necessary to promote the novice to orders, a dispensation from the prohibition of Canon 567, § 2, would be needed.

Before the novice is admitted to profession, he is to present to the superior a written petition in which the candidate expressly declares his vocation to the religious and clerical state, and proclaims his firm resolve to devote himself perpetually to clerical

---

[113] Cf. Pius XI, ep. ap. "*Unigenitus Dei Filius,*" 19 mart. 1924—*AAS,* XVI (1924), 142.

[114] Canon 567, § 2; S. C. de Religiosis, instr. "*Quantum religiones,*" 1 dec. 1931, n. 14—*AAS,* XXIV (1932), 79.

[115] *Glossa ordinaria* ad c. 3, *de privilegiis,* V, 7, in VI°, s.v. *convolaverint.*

[116] S. C. Ep. et Reg., 4 nov. 1892, n. 1—*Fontes,* n. 2020.

[117] S. C. Ep. et Reg., *Cenomanen.,* 9 ian. 1895—Appeltern, *Compendium Praelectionum Juris Regularis* (2. ed., Parisiis, 1913), p. 77.

[118] Cf. canon 964, 2°, 4°.

[119] Larraona, "Commentarium Codicis"—*CpRM,* XXV (1944-1946), 24-25.

work in the religious life. This petition is to be kept in the archives.[120]

Although this document is referred to as a petition, the instruction *Quantum religiones* indicates only the two statements to be made by the novice, viz., of his vocation to the clerical state and religious life, and of his firm resolve to perpetually serve in this religious-clerical state. From the context, however, it seems that the petition is already a request for the reception of tonsure and minor orders, even though this is expressed but implicitly in the two declarations contained in the document. Since the Sacred Congregation has furnished no sample form for this first petition, the form customary in the various religious institutes can be used, provided that the necessary information is included. It is not necessary that this petition duplicate the request to make profession, but the two can well be combined into a single petition.[121]

ARTICLE IV. TEMPORARY PROFESSION AND MINOR ORDERS

After the candidate has made his temporary profession, he ordinarily enters upon the study of philosophy and theology in preparation for the priesthood. The present law requires that he engage in the study of philosophy for at least two years, in the study of sacred theology for at least four years.[122] These studies are to be made in houses in which a perfect common life is observed, for otherwise the candidate may not be promoted to orders.[123] Although each clerical religious institute should provide its own house of studies, superiors are given considerable latitude in making practical arrangements.[124] The entire course of studies,

---

[120] S. C. de Religiosis, instr. "*Quantum religiones,*" 1 dec. 1931, n. 14—*AAS,* XXIV (1932), 79.

[121] Several formulae are suggested by authors. Cf. Coronata, *De Sacramentis,* II, Appendix III, Formula XIII, a. Beste (*Introductio,* p. 527) seems to require more from the novice than does the Instruction, since his one formula embodies the sample given by the Sacred Congregation for major orders; this original document is ratified by the candidate before solemn vows or the subdiaconate.

[122] Canon 589, § 1.

[123] Canon 587, § 2.

[124] Canon 587, § 1, 3, 4.

which is under the supervision of a spiritual prefect, should be carried out in a thoroughly religious atmosphere, so that the devout practices which are characteristic to the particular institute and to religious are properly performed.[125] Not only should the customary ascetical means be employed,[126] but distracting occasions, such as arise from the reading of trivial books and periodicals, from partaking in indecorous sports,[127] from needless visits and travels,[128] and from assignments which hinder studies and school work, should be avoided.[129]

If the humanities were not finished before the novitiate, they are to be completed before the study of philosophy is begun, which in turn should be completed before the theological course.[130]

Although the curriculum at present resembles that of diocesan seminaries,[131] the Sacred Congregation of Religious has instituted a Commission on Studies to prescribe more exactly the educational program for religious.[132]

If the course of philosophy was begun immediately after the novitiate and extends only over two years, the religious will normally enter on his theological course during the last year of his triennial profession. He may be advanced to tonsure and minor orders at this time, after the superior has made the required investigations and a favorable report is received.[133]

Four factors are to be taken into consideration for the determining of the time when a candidate may be promoted to orders:

---

[125] Canon 588.

[126] Canon 595.

[127] S. C. de Religiosis, inst. "*Quantum religiones,*" 1 dec. 1931, n. 7—*AAS,* XXIV (1932), 76.

[128] *Ibid.,* n. 9—*AAS,* XXIV (1932), 77.

[129] Canon 589, § 2.

[130] Pius XI, ep. ap. "*Unigenitus Dei Filius,*" 19 mart. 1924—*AAS,* XVI (1924), 143; S. C. de Religiosis, instr. "*Quantum religiones,*" 1 dec. 1931, n. 5—*AAS,* XXIV (1932), 75-76.

[131] Cf. Canon 1365.

[132] Decr. 24 ian. 1944—*AAS,* XXXVI (1944), 213-214. One of the first acts was the preparation of a questionnaire to ascertain the present practice. Cf. *Periodica,* XXXIII (1944), 245-250.

[133] S. C. de Religiosis, instr. "*Quantum religiones,*" 1 dec. 1931, n. 14—*AAS,* XXIV (1932), 79-80.

his religious profession, his chronological age, his progress through the curriculum of studies, and the observance of the interstices. If the obligation imposed by even one of these factors is not satisfied, even though the other requirements have been met, the candidate may not be licitly promoted to orders. The fact that all of these requisites have been fulfilled does not guarantee, on the other hand, that the candidate will be promoted. Hence they are here considered as minimum essentials to the ordination of the religious.

While the candidate is in the period of temporary vows which are required before he may pronounce perpetual vows, he may be promoted only to tonsure and minor orders.[134] After simple profession as a prelude to solemn vows had been introduced under Pope Piux IX (1846-1878),[135] superiors were allowed to grant dimissorial letters on behalf of those in simple vows for tonsure and minor orders only.[136] For the prohibition of Pope Pius V (1566-1572) against the ordination of religious in simple vows to major orders with the title of poverty[137] applied also to Regulars who prefaced their solemn profession with a period of three years in simple, though perpetual, vows.[138] The Code allows superiors to grant dimissorial letters for the promotion of their temporarily professed subjects to tonsure and minor orders only.

Ordinarily the period of temporal profession will extend over a space of three years. If the candidate will not reach the age of twenty-one in three years,[139] this temporary profession is to be made for the time necessary to reach that age. Should the superior see fit, he can prolong the period of temporary vows for not more than another three-year period.[140] During this time the candidate remains a religious in temporary vows, which are prefaced to his final profession, and may be promoted to tonsure and minor orders only.

---

134 Canon 964, 3°.

135 Const. "*Ad universalis,*" 7 febr. 1862—*Fontes,* n. 532; S. C. super Statu Regularium, litt. encycl. "*Neminem latet,*" 19 mart. 1857—*Fontes,* n. 4381.

136 S. C. super Statu Regularium, declar. 12 iun. 1858, VII—*Fontes,* n. 4383.

137 Const. "*Romanus Pontifex,*" 12 oct. 1568—*Fontes,* n. 129.

138 S. C. super Statu Regularium, 20 ian. 1860, ad 1—*Fontes,* n. 4385.

139 Canon 573.

140 Canon 574.

If a portion or all of the theological course was completed before the candidate entered the novitiate, he is nevertheless obliged to await final profession before he may receive major orders. For, even though he is only in temporary vows, he is an exempt religious. Hence no bishop may ordain him without dimissorial letters from the religious superior, who, however, is forbidden to grant them for promotion to major orders of a subject temporarily professed.[141] The opinion which holds that an exempt religious who is only temporarily professed can be promoted to major orders with the dimissorial letters of a bishop[142] seems an unwarranted conclusion and contrary to canon 964, 2°.[143] Further evidence against this view can be gathered from the expression of the Holy See to allow, by means of a dispensation to be obtained in each case, that the religious anticipate final profession, with the consequent result that the superior can issue dimissorial letters for major orders in the normal manner.[144] Dispensations, as they are now granted, permit the religious to make his final profession twelve, and even eighteen, months before the temporary vows would expire. The religious must indicate that he is willing to accept the exception.[145]

Superiors of institutes in which the members do not make perpetual vows may not promote their subjects to sacred orders before the completion of three years of temporary vows. In institutes in which the members take no vows, dimissorials for major orders must await the making of the perpetual and final choice, if such is made, but in no case until after the candidate has spent

---

[141] Canon 964, 2°-3°.

[142] Fanfani, *De Iure Religiosorum ad Norman Codicis Iuris Canonici,* n. 285; Pejška, *Ius Canonicum Religiosorum* (3. ed., Friburgi Brisgoviae, 1927), p. 304.

[143] Cappello, *De Sacra Ordinatione,* n. 344, 3.

[144] Cf. S. C. Ep. et Reg., decr. *"Auctis admodum,"* 4 nov. 1892, n. 2—*Fontes,* n. 2020.

[145] Sartori, *Jurisprudentia,* pp. 37-38. It also seems proper that the vote of the council or chapter which is taken before the candidate is admitted to this final profession (canon 575, § 2) should be sought before the petition to anticipate profession is sent to the Holy See. Cf. S. C. Ep. et Reg., dubium, 26 ian. 1903—*Acta Sanctae Sedis* (41 vols., Romae, 1865-1908), XXXV (1902-1903), 664-665 (hereafter cited *ASS*).

three full years from the time of his acceptance into the institute.[146] In all cases, then, unless a special dispensation is received, a religious may not be promoted to major orders within the first three years of religious life.

The second factor affecting the promotion of religious to orders involves the chronological age of the candidate. Since a definite age is specified only for the major orders, it does not enter into the consideration for tonsure and the minor orders.

The third factor is the completion of the required courses of study. Tonsure may not be conferred before the theological course has been begun.[147] This is usually the pertinent condition which determines when a religious will be promoted to orders. Because of the confusion in the opinions of canonists regarding the status of a religious who has been promoted to tonsure and minor orders but has not yet made his final profession, some institutes regularly defer all ordinations until after the final profession, even though the candidate has already begun his theological studies. There is no law urging the reception of tonsure and minor orders when the study of theology is begun. Until the religious has received clerical tonsure, however, he is not strictly obliged to attend the monthly theological conference,[148] for without tonsure he is not a cleric.[149]

The fourth factor which determines the time of ordination is the law of interstices. The determination of the interval between tonsure and the order of porter, and between the several minor orders, is left to the prudent judgment of the bishop.[150]

Religious, just as secular candidates, were obliged to observe the law of interstices.[151] Since no exception is made in the present

---

[146] S. C. de Religiosis, instr. "*Quantum religiones,*" 1 dec. 1931, n. 15—*AAS,* XXIV (1932), 80.

[147] Canon 976, § 1.

[148] Canon 591.

[149] Canon 108, § 1.

[150] Canon 978, § 2.

[151] S. C. C., *Mediolanen.,* anno 1573—Benedictus XIV (Prosper de Lambertinis), *Institutiones Ecclesiasticae* (Romae, 1747), LVIII, 3-5; Gasparri, *De Sacra Ordinatione,* n. 507; Many, *Praelectiones de Sacra Ordinatione* (Parisiis, 1905), n. 167 (hereafter cited *De Sacra Ordinatione*).

legislation, the basic obligation to observe them remains unchanged. While the power to dispense from the interstices is vested in the ordaining bishop, he is to defer to the causes proposed to him by the religious superior.[152] If the religious superior himself ordains, as in the case of an abbot, the power to dispense from the interstices is vested in him.[153]

Since the interval between the various minor orders is not specified but left to the prudent judgment of the bishop, who in the case of religious is to acquiesce to the religious superior, the presentation of a candidate for such orders can be interpreted that the superior considers the time since the last ordination of sufficient duration.

Candidates for promotion to tonsure and minor orders are to make a spiritual retreat for at least three days.[154] Before the Code, except for the period between the years 1682 and 1710, a retreat was not prescribed by pontifical law as a preparation for tonsure and minor orders. Pope Alexander VII (1655-1667) required that in the city of Rome and the six suburbicarian sees candidates for sacred orders make a retreat for ten days.[155] Pope Innocent XI (1676-1689) extended this legislation to all of Italy, and further required a retreat of the same duration to be made by candidates for minor orders too;[156] however this latter provision was modified under Pope Clement XI (1700-1721), so that only candidates for major orders were bound to the retreat.[157] Although Regulars were not bound to this legislation, they were urged to

---

[152] S. C. C., *Aquen.*, mense iul. 1589—*Fontes,* n. 2209; *Brugnaten.*, 17 maii 1593—*Fontes,* n. 2257; *Nullius,* 31 maii 1597—*Fontes,* n. 2311; *Savonen.*, 1 iul. 1597—*Fontes,* n. 2316; 12 sept. 1609—*Fontes,* n. 2379; *Miden.*, 23 aug. 1686, ad 8—*Fontes,* n. 2895; Cappello, *De Sacra Ordinatione,* n. 420; Coronata, *De Sacramentis,* II, n. 79.

[153] S. C. C., *Fanen.*, 6 iul. 1592—Gasparri, *De Sacra Ordinatione,* n. 507.

[154] Canon 1001, § 1.

[155] Const. *"Apostolica sollicitudo,"* 7 aug. 1662, § 2-4—*Fontes,* n. 239.

[156] S. C. Ep. et Reg., encycl. (ad Ep. Italiae), 9 oct. 1682—*Fontes,* n. 1812.

[157] S. C. C., ep. encycl., 1 febr. 1710—Ferraris, *Prompta Bibliotheca Canonica, Iuridica, Moralis, Theologica, necnon Ascetica, Polemica, Rubricistica, Historica* (ed. noviss., 9 vols., Romae, 1885-1899), s.v. *Exercitia Spiritualia,* n. 2 (hereafter cited *Bibliotheca*).

adopt the custom of a retreat before ordination.[158] The custom in Rome, nevertheless, was that Regulars prefaced their promotion to each sacred order with a retreat of ten days.[159] Religious are now considered bound to a retreat as are other candidates.[160]

The Code establishes the requisite of a retreat for a minimum of three full days for tonsure and each minor order, unless several orders are conferred on the same or successive days.[161] By analogy to the declaration of the Sacred Congregation of the Sacraments,[162] if three full days cannot be prefaced to each minor order, the time of a three days' retreat should precede the first ordination, and at least one day should intervene between that and each subsequent ordination.[163]

The place of the retreat for religious will normally be their own religious house, unless the religious superior designates another. An attestation that the retreat has been made is to be included, at least implicitly, in the dimissorial letters.[164] If for any reason the ordination is postponed more than six months after the retreat was made, the exercises should be repeated; if the time is less than six months, the major superior, in his capacity as an ordinary, determines whether or not a repetition is necessary.[165]

Before Regulars pronounce their solemn vows, they are to make a declaration, under oath, in which they petition for the order of subdiaconate and state: a) that they are not receiving that major order under any force or compulsion, but freely seek to embrace it and the obligations attached to it; b) that they are fully aware of the obligations which flow from that sacred order, accept them, and resolve, with the help of God, to ever keep them;

---

[158] Benedictus XIV, *Institutiones Ecclesiasticae,* CIV, n. 10-15; *idem, De Synodo Dioecesana* (2 vols., Romae, 1806), lib. XI, cap. 2, n. 16.

[159] Gasparri, *De Sacra Ordinatione,* n. 767; Many, *De Sacra Ordinatione,* n. 155.

[160] Coronata, *De Sacramentis,* II, n. 194; Cappello, *De Sacra Ordinatione,* n. 554. Canon 1001, § 3, also implies the obligation.

[161] Coronata, *loc. cit.*

[162] *Romana et aliarum,* 2 maii 1928—*AAS,* XX (1928), 359. Cf. *infra,* p. 42.

[163] Cappello, *De Sacra Ordinatione,* n. 552, 5°; Regatillo, *Ius Sacramentarium* (2 vols., Santander: Sal Terrae, 1946), II, n. 151.

[164] Canon 1001, § 3-4.

[165] Canon 1001, § 2.

c) that they clearly understand all that is prescribed by the vow of chastity and the law of celibacy, and intend, with God's help, to observe these obligations; and d) that they sincerely promise always to obey, according to the sacred canons, in all things which are commanded by their superiors in conformity with the discipline of the Church, and that they are prepared to give a good example in deed and word, in order to be worthy of receiving the reward promised by God.[166] Religious other than Regulars are to make this same sworn statement before receiving the order of subdiaconate.

Should the religious, after receiving major orders, petition that a process be instituted to obtain a declaration of freedom from the obligations of sacred orders, it seems that this sworn statement is to be introduced into the trial after the manner of contrary evidence.[167]

ARTICLE V. PERPETUAL PROFESSION AND MAJOR ORDERS

By perpetual profession, the religious not only becomes permanently fixed as a member of his institute, but also acquires a definite status in respect to ordination. One of the direct effects is the assignment of a canonical title.

Regulars who have pronounced solemn vows enjoy the title of solemn religious profession, or, as it is sometimes called, the title of poverty.[168] This title seems to stem from the legislation of the Council of Chalcedon (451), which allowed priests and deacons to be ordained for the church of a monastery.[169] Although gradually more and more monks were promoted to sacred orders, the permanent bond which the Regular entered into with his order assured his support. Hence there was no need for the corrective legislation which was necessary for the other canonical titles.

---

[166] S. C. de Religiosis, instr. *"Quantum religiones,"* 1 dec. 1931, n. 17-18—*AAS*, XXIV (1932), 80-81. Cf. Appendix, *infra*, p. 133.

[167] Cf. S. C. de Sacramentis, decr. 9 iun. 1931, Appendix, XVIII—*AAS*, XXIII (1931), 471. At the time these *Regulae* were published, the instruction *"Quantum religiones"* had not yet appeared. They make mention, therefore, only of the sworn statement made by secular clerics.

[168] Canon 982, § 1.

[169] Canon 6—Mansi, VII, 394-395; c. 1, D. LXX.

Pope Pius V (1566-1572) specifically recognized the title of poverty and restricted its use exclusively to Regulars who had made solemn vows.[170] The restricted use of this title continues in the Code.

Members of congregations in which perpetual vows are taken acquire the title of the common table, or of the congregation, as is specified in their constitutions.[171] Titles of this kind developed as a result of special indults to religious of simple perpetual vows, who were not allowed to use the title of poverty.[172] Although before the Code the title of common table, or its equivalent, could be used only by those institutes to whom it had been granted by indult,[173] it is now allowed by common law to all religious congregations in which the members make perpetual vows.[174]

Actually, the titles of both Regulars and perpetually professed religious differ only in their historical basis. In any case, however, the religious who is to be ordained with either title must have made solemn or simple perpetual profession before he can use it.[175]

All other religious are to be ordained with one of the titles used for secular clerics,[176] such as the title of a benefice, patrimony, or pension, or service of the diocese or mission.[177] In this group are included religious who take only temporary vows and mem-

---

[170] Const. "*Romanus Pontifex,*" 14 oct. 1568—*Fontes,* n. 129.

[171] Canon 982, § 2.

[172] Many, *De Sacra Ordinatione,* n. 189; Gasparri, *De Sacra Ordinatione,* n. 587. Thus the Congregation of the Most Holy Redeemer (Redemptorists) received such a grant from Pope Leo XII (1823-1829) in his constitution "*Inter religiosas,*" 11 mart. 1828, § 2—*Bullarii Romani Continuatio Summorum Pontificum* (19 vols., Prati, 1756-1883), VIII, 660 (hereafter cited *Bull. Rom. Cont.*).

[173] S. C. Ep. et Reg., dubium, 12 febr. 1894, ad 3—*ASS,* XXVI (1893-1894), 619-620.

[174] Augustine, *A Commentary on the New Code of Canon Law* (3. ed., 8 vols., St. Louis, Mo.: Herder, 1920-1931), IV, 475 (hereafter cited *Commentary*); Coronata, *De Sacramentis,* II, n. 94.

[175] Regatillo, *Ius Sacramentarium,* II, n. 99; Cappello, *De Sacra Ordinatione,* n. 428, 3; Coronata, *De Sacramentis,* II, n. 94.

[176] Canon 982, § 3.

[177] Canon 979, § 1; 981, § 1.

bers of such institutes in which no vows at all are taken. No difficulty will arise if the religious can provide a benefice, patrimony, or pension which can guarantee his support. Since, however, the use of these titles is in practice so infrequent, a problem arises when they are ordained for the service of the diocese or mission. As religious they are subject to their religious superior, who may change their assignment so that they would not be serving the diocese or mission for which they were ordained. Also, should they ever leave the institute, the bishop is bound to provide for their support. The difficulty is solved in practice by obtaining an indult from the Holy See for the use of a title similar to that of perpetually professed religious.[178]

After the religious has made his profession of perpetual vows,[179] his perpetual or final choice, or, in institutes in which these are not made, after at least three years from the time of his acceptance into the institute, he may be promoted to major orders when and as the other requirements are satisfied.[180] Once again the three other factors of the age of the religious, the completion of his studies, and the intervals determined by the law of interstices must be considered as determining the time when orders may be received.

If the candidate is not a Regular, he is to make the declaration and petition concerning major orders and the obligations they impose before receiving the order of subdiaconate.[181] It may be noted that only one such sworn statement is required of religious, and that before the subdiaconate,[182] even though seculars are required to present a similar petition and declaration before each major order.[183] Since the religious superior is obliged to ascertain

---

[178] Regatillo, *Ius Sacramentarium,* II, n. 99; Coronata, *De Sacramentis,* II, n. 95.

[179] Canon 964, 3°.

[180] S. C. de Religiosis, instr. "*Quantum religiones,*" 1 dec. 1931, n. 15—*AAS,* XXIV (1932), 80.

[181] Cf. *supra,* p. 34.

[182] S. C. de Religiosis, instr. "*Quantum religiones,*" 1 dec. 1931, n. 17-18—*AAS,* XXIV (1932), 80-81.

[183] S. C. de Sacramentis, instr. "*Quam ingens,*" 27 dec. 1930, § 3. n. 1—*AAS,* XXIII (1931), 124.

that the candidate is making a free choice in receiving ordination, he seems to be able to insist that his subjects present a written petition before each ordination.[184]

The chronological age of the candidate must correspond to the minimum established for each of the major orders, viz., twenty-one years for the subdiaconate, twenty-two for the diaconate, and twenty-four for the priesthood.[185] Since perpetual profession cannot be validly[186] made until after the candidate has completed his twenty-first year,[187] no difficulty because of age will arise for the subdiaconate, which can not be licitly conferred before perpetual profession.

If the candidate has completed his studies but has not attained his twenty-fourth year, the Holy See may be requested to grant a dispensation from the law regarding the requisite age.[188] These dispensations are granted for promotion to the priesthood, and no mention is made of a dispensation for the other major orders.

The course of studies completed by the ordinand is generally the most decisive factor for determining the time at which a religious will be promoted to orders. By common law, the subdiaconate is to be conferred at the end of the third year of the theological course, the diaconate at the beginning of the fourth year, and the priesthood only in the latter half of the fourth year.[189] Pope Clement VIII (1592-1605) had required at least three years of study after profession before a religious was to receive his ordination.[190] Under Pope Leo XIII (1878-1903), the time periods at which major orders were to be conferred on religious were specified as the completion of the first, second, and third year of

[184] Coronata, *De Sacramentis,* II, p. 342, footnote 3.

[185] Canon 975.

[186] Canon 572, § 1, 1°.

[187] Canon 573.

[188] Sartori, *Jurisprudentia,* p. 67. The quinquennial faculties granted by the Sacred Congregation of Religious allow the local ordinary to dispense even exempt religious from the lack of age for the priesthood. This dispensation can cover a deficiency up to twelve months, and, if the candidate has neither received nor needs any other dispensation, for as many as sixteen months. Cf. Bouscaren, *The Canon Law Digest,* II, 36.

[189] Canon 976, § 2.

[190] Const. *"Cum ad regularem,"* 19 mart. 1603, § 20—*Fontes,* n. 189.

theological studies,[191] and the ordaining prelate was to see that this requirement was observed.[192]

With the introduction of the minimum requisite of four years of theological studies, the Sacred Congregation of Religious forbade acceleration of this time by longer class hours or studies continued through vacation periods. If the equivalent of three years of theological work had been completed in thirty months, the candidate was permitted to receive ordination; but the entire course, even in that event, was to extend over forty-five months, the vacation periods between the years of theological study included.[193]

For various reasons it sometimes becomes desirable to approach the Holy See for a dispensation from these time requirements in relation to theological study, in order that the candidate may be promoted to the priesthood before the established time.[194] The dispensation usually allows the order of priesthood to be received as early as the end of the third year of theology. The intention of the Sacred Congregation in making such a grant is that the other major orders be received within the course of the third year without need of another dispensation.[195] At present it is the practice not to dispense from the requirements of theological studies for ordination, unless the ordinand has reached his twenty-sixth year.[196]

The Holy See has granted to some religious institutes the indult or privilege whereby their members may be promoted to major orders earlier than is allowed by the common law.[197]

---

[191] S. C. Ep. et Reg., decr. *"Auctis admodum,"* 4 nov. 1892, n. 6—*Fontes,* n. 2020.

[192] Leo XIII, const. *"Conditae a Christo,"* 8 dec. 1900, § 2, VI—*Fontes,* n. 644.

[193] Declar. 7 sept. 1909—*Fontes,* n. 4397; dubia, 31 maii 1910—*Fontes,* n. 4402.

[194] Sartori, *Jurisprudentia,* pp. 66-67.

[195] Procura Generalis O.F.M.—*Acta Minorum,* LIII (1934), 351.

[196] S. C. de Religiosis, 15 ian. 1945—*Acta Minorum,* LXIV (1945), 14.

[197] Thus Pope Benedict XV (1914-1922) granted the Benedictine Order the privilege that solemnly professed monks might be promoted to major orders at the end of the first, second, and third year of theology respectively. Rescr. 24 febr. 1921—*Annales OSB,* XXVIII-XXXIV (1920-1926), 82-83.

When religious have been promoted to the priesthood before the completion of four years of theology, they are obliged to continue their studies until the minimum requirement of four years is satisfied. While they are thus finishing their course, it is forbidden that they be engaged in the ministry of souls, in preaching, in the hearing of confessions, and in the exterior works of the institute. The observance of these restrictions is a grave obligation of the superior.[198]

The observance of the interstices is the fourth factor which must be considered in the determining of the time when a religious may be promoted to the several major orders. These intervals are indicated more definitely for sacred orders than for minor orders. The order of subdiaconate may not be conferred until a year after the last of the minor orders was received. Between each of the major orders at least three months are to elapse. However, the bishop may shorten the intervals if in his judgment it would serve the needs or the utility of the Church.[199] If the program of required studies described in canon 976, in relation to the respective major orders, is observed as indicated, no difficulties in regard to the interstices will arise. However, the law itself allows considerable latitude to the prudent judgment of the bishop.

As has already been indicated, the jurisprudence of the Sacred Congregations vindicated the right to dispense from interstices to the ordaining bishop, who was to accept the judgment of the religious superior as to the cause for the dispensation.[200] In petitioning the bishop for the dispensation, the formula suggested is: *Rogamus te Reverendissime Domne ut dispensare digneris super Interstitia sicut et nos dispensamus.*[201]

Some orders and congregations obtained further the privilege whereby their superior received the power to dispense, or they were dispensed directly by the Roman Pontiff. Since these are special grants, they may be used according to the tenor of the

---

[198] S. C. de Religiosis, declar. 27 oct. 1923—*AAS,* XV (1923), 549.

[199] Canon 978, § 2.

[200] *Supra,* pp. 32-33.

[201] S. C. Ep. et Reg., *Ordinis Eremitarum Camaldulensium,* 13 iul. 1730—*Fontes,* n. 1847.

particular concession. Considerable confusion exists on precisely which religious institutes enjoy these special grants.[202]

Several other requisites must be satisfied before the religious candidate may be promoted to orders. These do not operate, however, to determine the time for ordination.

Under the common law before the promulgation of the Code it was held that all who were to be promoted to sacred orders should make a profession of faith.[203] Pope Pius X (1903-1914) required that the oath against modernism be taken by all who were to be ordained to sacred orders. This oath was to be preceded with the profession of faith.[204] The oath against modernism, to which the profession of faith was prefaced, was to be received by the proper prelate of the ordinand, who, in the case of religious, was not their religious superior, but the bishop who conferred the orders.[205] The ordaining bishop was to be understood as the bishop of the diocese in whose territory the ordination took place, even though he himself did not confer the orders. For it is in the diocesan bishop's jurisdiction that the minister ordains and it is in his place that the latter functions. The religious superior could not receive the profession of faith and witness the oath in his own name, but he could do so as a delegate of the bishop.[206] Before the Code, therefore, the oath against modernism, to which the profession of faith was prefaced, was to be received by the bishop of the diocese in whose territory the ordination of the religious took place.

---

[202] Ledwolorz, "De Regularium Privilegiis Recipiendi Sacros Ordines extra Tempora et Non Servatis Interstitiis"—*Antonianum* (Romae, 1926-), XX (1945), 432-438. Cf. Gannon, *The Interstices Required for the Promotion to Orders,* The Catholic University of America Canon Law Studies, n. 196 (Washington, D. C.: The Catholic University of America Press, 1944), 79-81; Capobianco, *Privilegia et Facultates Ordinis Fratrum Minorum,* n. 127-129.

[203] Canavan, *The Profession of Faith,* The Catholic University of America Canon Law Studies, n. 151 (Washington, D. C.: The Catholic University of America Press, 1942), p. 87. Cf. c. 6, D. XXIII.

[204] Motu propr. *"Sacrorum Antistitum,"* 1 sept. 1910—*Fontes,* n. 689.

[205] S. C. Consist., declar. 17 dec. 1910, ad I—*AAS,* III (1911), 25.

[206] Vermeersch, "Annotationes"—*Periodica,* V (1911), 272. Vermeersch originally had held that the religious superior received the oath in his own right. Cf. "Annotationes"—*Periodica,* V (1911), 210.

Although the Code requires only the profession of faith to be made,[207] the obligation of taking the oath against modernism remains in force.[208] While the Code requires the profession to be made before the local ordinary, it does not further specify this prelate. Since before the promulgation of the Code the profession of faith was made in conjunction with the oath against modernism, and this was to be made before the bishop of the diocese in whose territory the ordination took place, it seems proper to conclude that the local ordinary who is to receive the profession of faith is he in whose territory the orders are conferred. He may, of course, delegate the religious superior to actually witness the profession of faith and the oath.[209]

Although the motu proprio *Sacrorum Antistitum* required the oath for all major orders, it sufficed if it was taken once, and that before the subdiaconate;[210] the ordinary could require it to be made, however, before each of the major orders[211] by all candidates, even Regulars.[212] The Code requires the profession of faith only before the subdiaconate.[213]

The usual practice is to authorize the religious superior to act as delegate not only to witness the profession of faith but also to receive the oath against modernism.

The spiritual retreat which is to be made before each major order is to extend for a minimum of six days. If more than one major order is being received within six months, the retreat for the diaconate may be reduced by the ordinary to as few as three days.[214] The full time is to be spent in spiritual retreat even in those cases in which the major orders follow in close succession, as within the space of a month. Should major orders be conferred with such short intervals that the full time cannot be observed, as when orders follow on consecutive days, the first major order

---

[207] Canon 1406, § 1, 7°.

[208] S. C. S. Off., decr. 22 mart. 1918—*AAS*, X (1918), 136.

[209] Cf. Coronata, *Institutiones*, II, n. 970, footnote 8.

[210] S. C. Consist., declar. 25 sept. 1910, ad 2—*Fontes*, n. 2075.

[211] S. C. Consist., resp. 24 mart. 1911, ad 2—*AAS*, III (1911), 181.

[212] Vermeersch, "Annotationes"—*Periodica*, VI (1912), 27.

[213] Canon 1406, § 1, 7°.

[214] Canon 1001, § 1. Cf. *supra*, p. 34.

should be preceded with the minimum of a six-day retreat, the other sacred orders with at least a one-day retreat.[215] The determination of this reduced period of retreat, as well as that authorized by the Code for the diaconate when several major orders are received within six months, is reserved to the major superior in his capacity as an ordinary. He also decides whether the retreat is to be repeated if the ordination has been postponed, but not beyond six months.[216]

Even though a religious candidate has complied with these canonical requirements, he needs further to be selected for orders by the religious superior.

---

[215] S. C. de Sacramentis, *Romana et aliarum*, 2 maii 1928—*AAS*, XX (1928), 359.

[216] Canon 1001, § 1-2.

CHAPTER III

The Religious Superior

The rôle of the religious superior in the ordination of his subjects is comparable to that of a bishop in respect to his clergy. It is his duty to select apt candidates, provide them with a religious and clerical training, determine their fitness for orders, and finally authorize their ordination. Without hesitation Pope Pius XI (1922-1939) referred to religious superiors the same considerations he addressed to bishops on their obligations of preparing candidates for the clerical ministry.[1]

The authority and responsibility of the religious superior juridically resides in his exclusive competence to issue dimissorial letters for the ordination of his religious subjects. Without these letters no bishop may licitly ordain an exempt religious;[2] with dimissorial letters from the superior the minister is completely justified in ordaining those candidates who are presented to him as properly trained and worthy of promotion to orders. Though he has the right to examine the candidates, he is not bound to do so.[3] Therefore the Church has not only charged the superior with the selection of worthy candidates and their preparation for orders, but has also imposed upon him the obligation and entrusted to him the authority to prohibit the ordination of unsuitable candidates.

ARTICLE I. HISTORICAL DEVELOPMENT OF THE RIGHTS OF THE SUPERIOR

A hermit could be persuaded to accept ordination without a trespass on his obligation to any superior. But with the rise of

[1] Ep. encycl. *"Ad catholici sacerdotii,"* 20 dec. 1935—*AAS,* XXVIII (1936), 43-44.

[2] Canon 964, 2°.

[3] S. C. de Religiosis, instr. *"Quantum religiones,"* 1 dec. 1931, n. 12-13—*AAS,* XXIV (1932), 78-79.

cenobitic monasticism, the abbot was recognized to possess authority over the lives and actions of his subjects. Yet when monks were first admitted to the clerical state, this was done at the will of the bishop and without the seeking of the consent of the religious superior.[4]

The III Council of Arles (455) was convoked for the purpose of settling a dispute between Bishop Theodore and Abbot Faustus because of the ordination of one of the monks from the monastery at Lerins without a consultation of the abbot. It was decided that for the future the local bishop was to have the exclusive right to ordain monks in his territory, but that he was not to perform such ordinations unless he was asked by the abbot.[5]

Pope Gelasius I (492-496) insisted upon an examination of the past life of the monk who was a candidate for sacred orders,[6] though he did not require that this search be as thorough as that required in the case of a layman, since monastic life itself was a trial and proof of the candidate's fitness.[7] He prescribed, however, that the abbot under whom the monk lived was to request the ordination.[8]

The Council of Agde (506) forbade the ordination of vagrant monks unless they had the testimony of their abbot.[9] The Council of Carthage (535) stressed the need of the abbot's consent for the ordination of his monks.[10]

Most monastic rules made no provisions at all for the ordination of monks.[11] The Rule of Aurelianus, Bishop of Arles (546-549), provided for the ordination of whomsoever the abbot

---

[4] Hallier, *De Sacris Electionibus et Ordinationibus ex Antiquo et Novo Ecclesiae Usu* (in Migne, *Theologiae Cursus Completus,* Vol. XXIV, Parisiis, 1860), Pars I, sect. 3, Appendix (hereafter cited *De Sacris Electionibus*).

[5] Mansi, VII, 907-908.

[6] C. 1, D. LV; c. 8, D. LXXVII; Jaffé, n. 636.

[7] C. 9, D. LXXVII; Jaffé, n. 636.

[8] C. 28, C. XVI, q. 1; Jaffé, n. 697.

[9] C. 33, C. XVI, q. 1; Mansi, VIII, 329.

[10] Mansi, VIII, 842.

[11] Cf. Benedict of Aniane, *Concordia Regularum,* c. LXVII, LXIX—*PL,* CIII, 1313-1316, 1323-1326.

selected.[12] St. Benedict (ca. 480-ca. 543/547) charged the abbot, should he seek to have a monk ordained, to see that the candidate was worthy of the priesthood.[13]

Pope Gregory the Great (590-604) generally required the abbot's consent for the ordination of a monk, whether the priest so chosen was to serve in the monastery or elsewhere.[14] Pope Lucius III (1181-1185) forbade bishops to ordain religious unless their superior agreed to the ordination. For it was possible that hidden faults, known to the abbot, might be present. Hence the bishop was not to promote a religious, even though the latter already was in orders, for the bishop was not aware of the reasons why the superior refused to have the religious ordained to higher orders.[15] Even when Pope Clement V (1305-1314) provided for the ordination of all monks, he ordered that this be done at the behest of the abbot.[16]

Subsequent legislation sought rather to curb the power of the superior than to vindicate it. This very effort, however, implicitly recognized his right to authorize the ordination of his subjects.

The Clementine decree, which received its name after Pope Clement VIII (1592-1605) who authorized its publication, acknowledged the right of the religious superior to issue dimissorial letters for the promotion of his subjects to orders.[17] These letters were in themselves sufficient and did not need to be supplemented by others from any bishop.[18]

The present Code has clearly expressed this exclusive right, so that no exempt religious may be ordained without dimissorial letters from his major superior.[19]

[12] C. XL—*PL*, CIII, 1325.

[13] *Regula*, c. LXII.

[14] *Gregorii I Papae Registrum Epistolarum—Monumenta Germaniae Historica, Epistolarum Tomus I et II* (ediderunt Ewald et Hartmann, Berolini, 1891-1899), VI, 27; Jaffé, n. 1407; VIII, 17: Jaffé, n. 1504 (partially quoted as c. 1, D. LVIII); XIII, 11: Jaffé, n. 1875. Cf. c. 2, C. XVI, q. 1; c. 5, C. XVIII, q. 2

[15] C. 5, X, *de temporibus ordinationum et qualitate ordinandorum,* I, 11; Jaffé, n. 15198.

[16] C. 1, *de statu monachorum vel canonicorum regularium,* III, 10, in Clem.

[17] S. C. C., decr. 15 mart. 1596—*Fontes,* n. 2294.

[18] S. C. C., *Senonen.,* 28 febr. 1654, ad 9—*Fontes,* n. 2734.

[19] Canon 964, 2°.

ARTICLE II. THE COMPETENT SUPERIOR

By the law of the Code, an exempt religious may not be ordained by any bishop if he is not in possession of dimissorial letters from the candidate's proper major superior, whose right in this matter is exclusive. Under no circumstances, then, may a minister licitly, albeit validly, confer any order, even tonsure, without this authorization.[20] The competent superior for the granting of the dimissorial letters for the ordination of non-exempt religious will of necessity be determined from the indult or privilege from which is derived the right to grant letters at all. For this latter group, however, both the religious superior and the proper bishop seem capable of granting the letters.[21] Discussion at this time will of necessity be limited to exempt religious whose superiors, by law, enjoy the faculty to grant dimissorial letters.

The Code grants the power of preparing dimissorial letters to the major superior of the candidate. The law does not attempt to give a complete list by which major superiors are known in the various religious institutes, but its listing does provide a norm for comparison. The constitutions of the particular religious institute can more precisely indicate which of the superiors occupy their positions as major superiors.

For convenience in discussing the determination of the major superior, it will be of advantage to distinguish the various institutes into the decentralized and centralized types of internal organization. For problems which arise in reference to one group do not have their counterpart in the other.

In the decentralized type, the characteristic feature is the autonomy of each monastery from the others, even though a loose federation combines them into an association which has only limited authority. Most Benedictine monasteries are of this kind. The ruling superior of each independent house is the major superior who is competent to grant the dimissorial letters for the ordina-

---

[20] Augustine, *Commentary,* IV, 436.

[21] Cf. Cappello, *De Sacra Ordinatione,* n. 344, 5.

tion of the members of that house. Such superiors are the ruling abbots[22] and the conventual priors.[23]

The authority of the superior of the monastic congregation, which is a loose federation of independent monasteries, must be determined from the constitutions of that congregation. For though such superiors are major superiors, they possess only the rights granted through such constitutions or through particular decrees of the Holy See.[24] The Abbot Primate, though a major superior, has ordinary jurisdiction only in the abbey of St. Anselm.[25] Although he can ordain Benedictines studying at that house, they must present dimissorial letters from their abbot.[26] Hence the major superior competent to grant dimissorial letters for the ordination of religious belonging to a decentralized institute is the one who rules the house to which the candidate belongs.

In centralized institutes, which are by far more common, the principal feature is the hierarchic progression of superiors, the one possessing authority and control over his inferiors. The Code makes mention of major superiors in such institutes as of two levels, viz., the Supreme Moderator and the Provincial.[27] The Supreme Moderator has jurisdiction over all the members of the institute, the Provincial enjoys it only over those who are within his assignment. The constitutions of the individual institute must be examined if one is to discover the limitations on the power of these superiors.[28] Unless the constitutions rule otherwise, the Supreme Moderator is capable of granting dimissorial letters for the ordination of any member of the institute, which the Provincial can do so only for the religious who belong to a house which is subject to his authority.

---

[22] Canon 488, 8°.

[23] S. C. de Religiosis, declar. 12 dec. 1922, ad I—*Annales OSB,* XXVIII-XXXIV (1920-1926), 100-101. The claustral prior is an official of the abbot, not a superior. Cf. Beste, *Introductio,* p. 316.

[24] Canon 501, § 3.

[25] Leo XIII, litt. ap. "*Summum semper,*" 12 iul. 1893—*Fontes,* n. 619; S. C. Ep. et Reg., decr. 16 sept. 1893—*Fontes,* n. 2022.

[26] *Infra,* p. 71.

[27] Canon 488, 8°.

[28] Canon 502.

While no difficulty arises from the concurrence of authority over the candidate by the Supreme Moderator and the Provincial, there is a repugnance in the concept that a religious can be subject to two superiors of the same hierarchical grade or rank. This problem arises when one considers canon 995, § 1,[29] in connection with canon 965.[30] The Supreme Moderator, inasmuch as he has power over all the houses and religious of the institute, can certify that the candidate belongs to the *familia* of a house which is subject to him. The Provincial Superior, to whom is entrusted the rule of the religious house to whose *familia* the candidate belongs, likewise can make the same attestation. No other provincial can, of course, make the same claim, for it would be destructive of religious discipline and order if two superiors of the same grade or rank were equally competent over the same religious houses.

As will be demonstrated later, a real distinction must be made between residing at a religious house and belonging to the *familia* of a religious house. It is possible for a religious to belong to a *familia* of one house even though he actually resides elsewhere. The proper bishop for ordination is he in whose diocese is located the religious house to which the candidate belongs.[31] The Provincial Superior of the house at which such a candidate may be resident does not have the competency, therefore, to issue dimissorial letters for his ordination.[32]

The practical difficulty in such a case arises from the factor of the physical distance which may separate the candidate from the house to which he belongs, and, consequently, from the bishop who should perform the ordination. If travel is too difficult, the proper bishop can be asked to permit the ordination to take place

[29] Etiam Superior religiosus suis litteris dimissoriis non solum testari debet promovendum professionem religiosam emisisse et esse de familia domus religiosae sibi subditae, sed etiam de studiis peractis, deque aliis iure requisitis.

[30] Episcopus ad quem Superior religiosus litteras dimissorias mittere debet, est Episcopus dioecesis, in qua sita est domus religiosa, ad cuius familiam pertinet ordinandus.

[31] *Infra*, p. 94.

[32] Regatillo (*Ius Sacramentarium*, II, n. 61) prefers to grant the power of preparing dimissorial letters to the Provincial Superior of the house of residence, and thus seems to do violence to canon 995.

elsewhere.[33] It is possible also for the institute to enjoy a privilege or an indult of approaching another bishop when the candidate is studying away from the religious house to which he belongs.

It seems proper to conclude, then, that the only Provincial Superior capable of granting the dimissorial letters is he to whose care is committed the house of which the ordinand is a true member,[34] unless the institute has another arrangement which has been approved for it by the Holy See.

Since the Code makes no distinction between major superiors in clerical and non-clerical institutes, it appears that the major superior in an exempt institute, even though he himself is not a cleric, can validly and licitly prepare the dimissorial letters for the ordination of his subjects.[35]

Before the present Code, local and other minor superiors in some institutes were authorized to issue dimissorial letters. Before a decision can be made as to whether this faculty continues into the present time, since it is contrary to the discipline of the Code, the source of the authorization must be ascertained. If the faculty arose from a provision in the constitutions of the particular institute, it was abrogated by the Code since it was opposed to the law of the Code.[36] If, however, the constitutions retained this provision and were approved after the promulgation of the Code, the legislator thereby admitted the exception to the common norm. In that event the minor superior would continue to enjoy the right to issue dimissorial letters.[37] On the other hand, if the faculty originated as an indult or privilege before the Code, it continues in force without the necessity of any further approval, since no clause in the present law revokes such privileges or indults.[38] A local or minor superior can therefore be competent to issue dimissorial letters if the faculty

---

[33] Canon 966, § 1.

[34] Coronata, *De Sacramentis,* II, n. 181.

[35] Cappello, *De Sacra Ordinatione,* n. 344, 2; Regatillo, *Ius Sacramentarium,* II, n. 61; Beste, *Introductio,* p. 518.

[36] Canon 489.

[37] Regatillo, *Ius Sacramentarium,* II, n. 61; Cappello, *De Sacra Ordinatione,* n. 344, 2.

[38] Cf. canon 4. Coronata, *De Sacramentis,* II, n. 42; Cappello, *De Sacra Ordinatione,* n. 344, 2; Regatillo, *Ius Sacramentarium,* II, n. 61.

has been granted through a privilege or indult either before or after the promulgation of the Code, and also if the constitutions, provided these have been approved since the Code, authorize him to do so.

A superior becomes competent to grant dimissorial letters from the time he enters upon his office; he loses competence when he discontinues in his position. He, as well as his successors, can limit or recall dimissorial letters which have been granted, but, once granted, they remain valid even though the superior's incumbency in office has in the meantime lapsed.[39]

ARTICLE III. SELECTION OF CANDIDATES

By granting dimissorial letters for the ordination of a religious, the superior presents to the minister a subject whom he deems worthy of orders. Such a presentation can not be made unless the superior is satisfied that the religious possesses the necessary qualities, and has satisfied the prescribed requisites for orders. Hence the superior has the duty and obligation not only of providing the necessary training, but also of selecting candidates worthy of promotion to orders.[40]

The selection of candidates for ordination begins in the years which precede even the novitiate. Already at that time a suitable training in piety and studies is to be given to such aspirants as have been prudently and deliberately selected with a view to their future state.[41] Especially before their admission to the novitiate an individual and painstaking inquiry is to be made, so that there will be admitted those alone who give signs of a vocation and who furnish a reason for the hope that they will be employed with profit in the ministry. To this end the testimonial letters are obtained. But should these be insufficient to reveal the true character of the applicant, further information from trustworthy sources should supplement them. The candidate's family too is to be investigated,

---

[39] Canon 963.

[40] S. C. de Religiosis, instr. "*Quantum religiones*," 1 dec. 1931, n. 12-13—*AAS*, XXIV (1932), 78-79.

[41] S. C. de Religiosis, instr. "*Quantum religiones*," 1 dec. 1931, n. 5—*AAS*, XXIV (1932), 75.

in order that there may be discovered any such proclivity to vices which may appear in the offspring. The signs of a vocation to the religious life alone are not sufficient, but indications of the applicant's fitness for the clerical state as well must be present.[42]

During the course of the novitiate, the religious superior will command an opportunity to observe the character and habits of the future cleric. It seems proper that when the novice master prepares his reports on the progress of the novice, concern should be had for those indications too which experience recognizes as favorable omens of a fruitful clerical vocation.[43]

After simple profession the religious may be promoted to tonsure and minor orders when the other requisites of the law have been satisfied.[44] This ordination cannot be authorized, however, until after the superior has made a thorough investigation of the candidate's morals, piety, modesty, chastity, inclination to the clerical state, progress in the necessary studies, and advance in the observance of religious discipline.[45]

The source of the necessary information is normally the spiritual prefect and the others who have intimate contact with the candidate. Since the spiritual prefect is charged with the care and training of the professed during their years of preparation,[46] he will be thoroughly acquainted with the life and ways of his charges. His testimony therefore merits considerable weight, especially if the superior who issues the dimissorial letters is not himself personally acquainted with the candidate. The several instructors

---

[42] S. C. de Religiosis, instr. "*Quantum religiones,*" 1 dec. 1931, n. 6—*AAS,* XXIV (1932), 76.

[43] Cf. canon 563.

[44] *Supra,* pp. 28 ff.

[45] S. C. de Religiosis, instr. "*Quantum religiones,*" 1 dec. 1931, n. 14—*AAS,* XXIV (1932), 79. The matter and method of this examination are more adequately treated by Gallagher, *The Examination of the Qualities of the Ordinand,* The Catholic University of America Canon Law Studies, n. 195 (Washington, D. C.: The Catholic University of America Press, 1944), pp. 99-118.

[46] Canon 588, § 1. For a further study on the spiritual prefect, cf. Gill, *The Spiritual Prefect in Clerical Religious Houses of Study,* The Catholic University of America Canon Law Studies, n. 216 (Washington, D. C.: The Catholic University of America Press, 1945).

too will know quite well the dispositions of the religious, and, whether they report directly or through the spiritual prefect, their testimony will enable the superior to reach a decision on the fitness of the candidate for ordination.[47]

The prefect, and other persons consulted, may reveal information possessed entirely on the basis of external observations, even though these facts may be unknown to others. For not only are public facts to be considered, but also private and personal defects which indicate that the candidate is unsuitable for ordination.

In no way, however, may faults learned through a manifestation of conscience,[48] or anything known from the sacramental confession, be revealed.[49] If the spiritual prefect or another has received a manifestation of conscience from the candidate, the information must be treated with the greatest confidence. The knowledge may not be used as the basis of even a secret vote, but the priest who received the manifestation of conscience is permitted to take part in the balloting for the candidate's promotion to orders.[50]

If the person whom the superior consults about the candidate acts as the confessor of the ordinand, it seems proper that after the analogy to the seminary confessor, he abstain entirely from giving his vote.[51]

Upon gathering the information, the religious superior should carefully weigh the evidence received with due consideration to the prudence, sincerity, and mature judgment of the persons from whom the facts were obtained. A record of the investigation as well as the conclusions should be drawn up in suitable form and

---

[47] Coronata (*De Sacramentis,* II, Appendix III, Formulary XIII, d) provides a convenient formulary for this examination. The formula suggested by Cardinal Jorio for seminarians could, with proper adaptations, serve the purpose. Cf. Jorio, *Sacerdos Alter Christus: De Instructione pro Scrutinio ad Ordines Peragendo Commentarius* (Romae: Sindacato Italiano Arti Grafiche, 1933), pp. 117-119.

[48] Gill, *op. cit.,* p. 112.

[49] Canon 890. Cf. S. C. S. Off., instr. 9 iun. 1915—Bouscaren, *The Canon Law Digest,* I, 413-414.

[50] Goyeneche, "Consultationes"—*CpRM,* XVIII (1937), 94-95.

[51] Cf. canon 1361, § 3; Beste, *Introductio,* p. 405.

preserved in the archives. Further, the superior should personally or through a learned and prudent deputy, who can command the confidence of the young candidate, interrogate the ordinands to make certain that the religious are freely and deliberately seeking ordination in the religious life.[52]

Preceding the subdiaconate, another investigation is to be made by the superior. Whereas for tonsure and minor orders a well-founded conjecture that the candidate would in time be a worthy priest suffices, there must exist moral certainty based on positive arguments that the candidate is fit for major orders.[53] Once again the candidate's life and character are to be examined in the same manner and on the same points as was done before he was promoted to tonsure. A comparison made between the facts recorded in both inquiries will reveal the progress he has made. Care should be taken to discover genuine proof of the presence of the requisites for major orders. The trouble and burden of the investigation will have been in vain if the results of the inquiry are not interpreted according to the norms and requirements of the Church for a candidate to major orders. The record made of the results of these investigations should be added to those made on previous occasions, and kept in the archives.[54]

Before the religious is promoted to the diaconate and the priesthood, similar investigations are to be made, though these need not be as searching as those for the earlier ordinations. The religious superior in the meanwhile should remain alert to anything which would suggest a dubious or even an entirely absent vocation. Every such doubt is to be resolved only upon a thorough inquiry and after prudent consultation. Should the scrutiny evidence the absence of a vocation, or leave a serious doubt about it, ascent to further orders is to be forbidden, and the entire matter referred to the Sacred Congregation of Religious, which will in each case decide the proper course to follow.[55]

---

[52] S. C. de Religiosis, instr. "*Quantum religiones,*" 1 dec. 1931, n. 14—*AAS,* XXIV (1932), 79.

[53] Canon 973, § 1, 3.

[54] S. C. de Religiosis, instr. "*Quantum religiones,*" 1 dec. 1931, n. 16—*AAS,* XXIV (1932), 80.

[55] S. C. de Religiosis, instr. "*Quantum religiones,*" 1 dec. 1931, n. 20—*AAS,* XXIV (1932), 81.

The Code further requires of each candidate an examination about the order he is to receive, and of the candidates for major orders a further test on tracts in sacred theology. It is within the province of the bishops to determine the method, examiners, and theological tracts for the examination.[56] No difficulty arises when the diocesan bishop confers the orders, for then he has the right to examine the candidates, if not as the local ordinary, then as the ordaining bishop.[57] The problem arises when exempt religious approach another than their diocesan bishop. Though the ordaining bishop may examine the candidates, there then arises the question whether the local ordinary also has the right to examine them.

Some authors[58] apply to exempt religious the provision of canon 997, § 1, which assigns the conducting of the examination to the local ordinary who ordains in his own right or grants dimissorial letters. When another bishop than the local ordinary ordains, the attestation of the grantor of the dimissorial letters that the candidate was examined according to canon 997, § 1, may be accepted by him. Before such a statement can be made, however, the examination must have taken place according to canon 997, § 1, which prescribes that it be taken before the local ordinary. The conclusion seems to be that the exempt religious must approach the local ordinary for the examination, either because of the direct obligation of canon 997, § 1, or in order to make the attestation according to 997, § 2.

The proponents of another school,[59] however, maintain that exempt religious are not bound to approach the local ordinary for this examination, and that it belongs to the religious superior to conduct this examination. Canon 997, § 1, does not apply to ex-

---

[56] Canon 996.

[57] Canon 997.

[58] Wernz-Vidal, *Ius Canonicum* (7 vols. in 9, Romae: Apud Aedes Universitatis Gregorianae, 1923-1938), IV, i, n. 272; Beste, *Introductio,* p. 545; Augustine, *Commentary,* IV, 522-523.

[59] Cappello, *De Sacra Ordinatione,* n. 542; Coronata, *De Sacramentis,* II, n. 185; Regatillo, *Ius Sacramentarium,* II, n. 147; O'Brien, *The Exemption of Religious in Church Law* (Milwaukee: Bruce, 1942), p. 188; Gallagher, *The Examination of the Qualities of the Ordinand,* pp. 129-131.

empt religious, they argue, since by the privilege of exemption such religious are removed from the jurisdiction of the local ordinary except in those cases wherein their subjection is specified in the law. Now, canon 997, § 1, contains no indication that it includes exempt religious. Hence the law does not apply to exempt religious.

Another objection to the inclusion of exempt religious under the ruling of canon 997, § 1, is based on the history of the examination of religious ordinands. The Council of Trent (1545-1563) required that Regulars be not ordained without an examination by the bishop.[60] If the diocesan bishop was absent or for some other reason did not conduct an ordination, the Regulars were to be examined by the bishop who conferred the orders,[61] who, however, did not seem obliged to conduct the examination, but could accept the testimony of the superior.[62] Thus the pre-Code discipline did not concede the right to examine exempt candidates to the local ordinary, but allowed it to the ordaining bishop. Since the presumption favors the retention of the discipline from before the Code in cases where the present law appears doubtful,[63] the local ordinary does not in that capacity enjoy the right to examine exempt religious candidates for orders.

The text of canon 997, § 1, describes the local ordinary as the one who ordains in his own right or grants the dimissorial letters. The right to ordain is described as an alternative of the right to grant dimissorial letters. Although the diocesan bishop has the right to receive dimissorial letters for the ordination of exempt religious, this is not identical with the right to ordain exempt religious.[64] Since the local ordinary can neither ordain exempt religious in his own right nor grant dimissorial letters for their

---

[60] Sess. XXIII, *de ref.*, c. 12.

[61] S. C. C., decr. 15 mart. 1596—*Fontes*, n. 2294.

[62] Many, *De Sacra Ordinatione*, n. 162. Gasparri (*De Sacra Ordinatione*, n. 751, 756), though he held that Regulars must be examined by the bishop, indicated that the practice at Rome was to ask Regulars only about the last order to be received. Cf. S. C. Ep. et Reg., *Ordinis Eremitarum Camaldulensium*, 13 iul. 1730—*Fontes*, n. 1847.

[63] Canon 6, 4°.

[64] *Infra*, p. 67.

ordination, he does not seem to be able to claim the right of ordination.

Another supporting argument can be deduced from the Instruction *Quantum religiones,* which applies canon 997, § 2, to the attestation made by the religious superior, and excuses the bishop, before God and the Church, if he ordains on the testimony of the superior. However, the bishop's right to examine is clearly preserved.[65]

From these arguments it seems quite clear that the local ordinary cannot claim the right to conduct the examination given before the ordination of exempt religious. However, while this demonstrates the fact that the local ordinary cannot claim the right to conduct the examination, it does not satisfactorily prove that when the dimissorial letters contain the claim that the candidate was examined according to canon 997, § 1, an examination conducted by the religious superior is sufficient.

Should the ordaining bishop conduct an examination of the candidate and find the religious unsuitable for ordination, the normal procedure will be for the religious to spend further time in study and, at a later date, return for another trial. If the religious superior feels that the rejection was unfair, the course of action will depend on which bishop refused to ordain the candidate. When the diocesan bishop refuses to ordain the candidate, the superior may not direct the dimissorial letters to another bishop, but must have recourse to the Holy See.[66] For this does not constitute one of the cases allowed by law for approaching another bishop.[67] Should the rejection have been made by a bishop who does not enjoy the right to receive the dimissorial letters, the religious may be sent to another minister. It seems necessary, however, that in this latter case the refusal of the first bishop be made known to the alternate chosen.[68]

---

[65] S. C. de Religiosis, instr. 1 dec. 1931, n. 12—*AAS,* XXIV (1932), 78.

[66] S. C. C., 23 apr. 1604—Ferraris, *Bibliotheca,* s.v. "Ordo," § 3, n. 67; S. C. C., *Granatae,* 14 mart. 1620—Monacelli, *Formularium Legale Practicum Fori Ecclesiastici* (3 vols, Venetiis, 1736-1751), II, tit. XIII, formula IV, n. 29. Cappello, *De Sacra Ordinatione,* n. 344, 9.

[67] Cf. canon 966, § 1.

[68] Cf. canon 44, § 1.

Although the observance of these safeguards in the selection of candidates for ordination will never entirely remove the burden and responsibility of the religious superior, the many inquiries and examinations are precautions which will protect the clerical state and the religious life as far as the prudence and experience of centuries can avail.

ARTICLE IV. PROHIBITION TO ASCEND TO ORDERS

Before any candidate may be licitly ordained, he must, in the judgment of his proper ordinary, possess the qualities required by law.[69] While tonsure and minor orders may be conferred on those who give reason for the hope that they will one day be worthy priests, major orders require moral certainty, based on positive proof, that the candidate is a fit subject for ordination.[70] Since an absence of objections against the candidate is not sufficient proof of his fitness for sacred orders, the religious superior could not, in such a case, licitly issue dimissorial letters.

If there is not only lack of proof of the candidate's suitability, but even evidence to the contrary, the superior can[71] and even must forbid the ordination of such a religious.[72]

The right of the religious superior to prohibit his subject from seeking ordination was asserted by Pope Lucius III (1181-1185), who refused to allow a bishop to admit to orders religious to whom their superior had denied further ordination. The basis of this decision was the possibility of a secret crime known perchance to the superior, not however to the bishop.[73] The Council of Trent (1545-1563) retained and enlarged the scope of this power and added greater permanence to the decision of the superior.[74] The present law treats that power in canons 970 and 2222, § 2.

The major superior can forbid his clerics ascent to orders for

[69] Canon 968, § 1.

[70] Canon 973, § 1, 3.

[71] Canon 970.

[72] Canon 2222, § 2.

[73] C. 5, X, *de temporibus ordinationum et qualitate ordinandorum*, I, 11; Jaffé, n. 15198.

[74] Sess. XIV, *de ref.*, c. 1.

any canonical cause, even though it is occult.[75] The basis of this prohibition must be a canonical cause, that is, one that renders an ordination invalid or illicit,[76] in that it connotes a non-observance of the law's express requirements for orders.[77] For a valid ordination, the law requires that the candidate be baptized and a male; for a licit ordination, he must be free from irregularities and impediments and, in the judgment of his ordinary, be endowed with the requisite qualities.[78] There is further required for a licit ordination the previous reception of confirmation by the candidate, a manner of life consistent with the order to be received, the necessary age for the several orders, due knowledge, the reception of the preceding order, the observance of the law of interstices, a canonical title,[79] a due preparation by means of the prescribed spiritual retreat,[80] the profession of faith,[81] the oath against modernism,[82] the sworn declaration of his intention to accept and observe the obligations of the clerical state,[83] and the necessary type of religious profession for the order to be received.[84] The candidate must not be bound by any prohibition to receive orders, as results from censures.[85]

To be barred from the reception of orders, there need be no fault or guilt on the part of the candidate, but simply the presence of a canonical reason which makes the ordination illicit. The prohibition can be imposed by reason of a cause over which the ordinand has no control, and of which he may even be unaware.[86]

---

[75] Canon 970.

[76] Beste, *Introductio*, p. 524; Augustine, *Commentary*, IV, 450.

[77] Blat, *Commentarium Textus Codicis Iuris Canonici*, III, i, n. 320; Pejška, *Ius Canonicum Religiosorum*, p. 302.

[78] Canon 968, § 1.

[79] Canon 974.

[80] Canon 1001.

[81] Canon 1406, § 1, 7°.

[82] Pius X, motu prop. "*Sacrorum antistitum*," 1 sept. 1910—*Fontes*, n. 689; S. C. S. Off., decr. 22 mar. 1918—*AAS*, X (1918), 136.

[83] S. C. de Religiosis, instr. "*Quantum religiones*," 1 dec. 1931, n. 17-18—*AAS*, XXIV (1932), 80-81.

[84] Canon 964, 3°.

[85] Canon 2265, § 1, 3°; 2275, 3°; 2283.

[86] Cf. canon 968, § 2; 988.

On the other hand, if evidence points to even a probable delict, or to a delict certainly committed but against which a criminal judicial action or suit has been ruled out by way of legal prescription, the superior has not only the right but also the duty to prohibit the candidate from the reception of orders if his possession of fitness has not been duly established.[87] While canon 970 permits the superior to act, canon 2222, § 2, imposes upon him the obligation to forbid further ordinations; the former extends to all canonical reasons, the latter is restricted to delicts.

A probable delict is such as cannot be fully proved but can be established by the testimony of at least one trustworthy witness.[88] The statute of limitations imposes judicial strictures which vary with the nature of the delict involved.[89]

The authority to prohibit ascent to orders, as stated by canon 970, is extended to major superiors; in cases of delicts the power extends to religious superiors, even though they do not come under the concept of an ordinary.[90] The prohibition is imposed not as by a judge but as by a superior, so that a process is unnecessary. It is proper, however, that the injunction take the form of a written decree, not only to serve as a record of the action taken, but also to provide the legitimate basis for recourse, should the affected religious wish to employ that device.[91]

While the legislator gives these extensive powers to religious superiors, the equitable claims of the religious must also be respected. The superior may not therefore use his authority in an arbitrary manner and without a legally justifying cause.[92] Care should also be exercised that the prohibition does not bring about the defamation of the candidate.[93] Though the superior is not

---

[87] Canon 2222, § 2.

[88] Augustine, *Commentary,* VIII, 87, footnote 10.

[89] Cf. canon 1703.

[90] Noval, "De Ratione Corrigendi ac Puniendi," III—*Jus Pontificium* (Romae, 1921-), III (1923), 208-210. Cf. Pistocchi, "De Superiore Potestatem Coactivam Habente"—*Il Monitore Ecclesiastico* (Romae, 1876-), IL (1937), 38-39.

[91] Coronata, "Pene e Procedimenti 'ad modum praecepti' "—*Perfice Munus!* (Taurini, 1926-), VII (1932), 353-354.

[92] Pejška, *Ius Canonicum Religiosorum,* p. 302.

[93] Vermeersch-Creusen, *Epitome,* III, n. 412.

bound to reveal the cause of the injunction to the candidate,[94] the latter may have recourse to the Supreme Moderator of the institute and to the Sacred Congregation for Religious. If the causes for the prohibition are not canonical, certain, and exact, the Holy See will not uphold the prohibition.[95]

Should a candidate, although once rejected for orders by his superiors, appear worthy of ordination after a sufficient amendment, he may be promoted to orders.[96]

ARTICLE V. THE DIMISSORIAL LETTERS

The granting of the dimissorial letters by the religious superior is the chief characteristic which distinguishes the discipline for the ordination of exempt religious from that of the seculars.[97] Without such letters no bishop can licitly promote an exempt religious to any order.[98] While of themselves the dimissorials confer no power of orders on the candidate, from the juridical point of view they are the equivalent of the exercise of the right of ordination. The candidate for whom they are prepared must be a fit subject for orders at the time the letters are granted. However, dimissorial letters are necessary for a valid ordination only in those cases wherein the minister, inasmuch as he is only an extraordinary minister of orders, cannot validly ordain another's subject who does not present dimissorials from his proper prelate.

The primary and basic concept of dimissorial letters is the authorization extended by a competent superior to a minister of orders in virtue of which the latter is permitted to ordain a candi-

---

[94] S. C. C., *Vercellen.*, 21 mart. 1643, ad 4—*Fontes,* n. 2642.

[95] Villien, "L'Ordination"—*Le Canoniste Contemporaine* (Parisiis, 1878-1922; 1924-1926, *Le Canoniste*), XLV (1922), 196.

[96] S. C. C., *Amalphitana,* 13 iul. 1765—Pallottini, *Collectio Omnium Conclusionum et Resolutionum Quae in Causis Propositis apud Sacram Congregationem Cardinalium S. Concilii Tridenti Interpretum Prodierunt ab Eius Institutione Anno MDLXIV ad Annum MDCCCLX, Distinctis Titulis Alphabetico Ordine per Materias Digesta* (17 vols., Romae, 1868-1893), s.v. "Sacramentum Ordinis," IV, n. 79 (hereafter cited Pallottini).

[97] Vermeersch-Creusen, *Epitome,* II, n. 182.

[98] Canon 964, 2°.

date who is not his subject.[99] Indirectly, dimissorial letters are also testimonials of the fitness of the candidate for orders.[100] Since a candidate may not be licitly promoted to orders unless he has the necessary qualities, the religious superior is not allowed to present for ordination a religious who is not fit. For, in the very act of authorizing the promotion to orders, the superior implies that he is satisfied that the requisite qualities are present and that the canonically prescribed formalities have been fulfilled. The legislator has placed the burden of ascertaining the fitness of a religious candidate on the religious superior. The ordaining prelate has no need for testimonials from any other source,[101] and can place full trust in and reliance on the sense of responsibility of the grantor of the letters.[102] In fact, if no doubt arises in the mind of the ordaining bishop, he should ordinarily not question the documents; even if a doubt arises, he can without investigation solve it in favor of the superior.[103]

Because of this indirect purpose of the dimissorial letters, the Code indicates several items in particular which are to be expressed in them, viz., the fact of the candidate's religious profession, of his membership in a house subject to the superior who grants the letters, of the completion of the required studies, and of the fulfillment of the other legal requirements.[104] The attestation in these letters that the spiritual retreat has been made seems likewise to be indicated.[105] Finally, the superior is also now required to state that the declarations which are to be made by the candidate be-

[99] Gasparri, *De Sacra Ordinatione*, n. 706; Many, *De Sacra Ordinatione*, n. 60; Cappello, *De Sacra Ordinatione*, n. 341, 9.

[100] Gasparri, *De Sacra Ordinatione*, n. 886; Many, *De Sacra Ordinatione*, n. 64; Cappello, *De Sacra Ordinatione*, n. 344; Regatillo, *Ius Sacramentarium*, II, n. 146; Coronata, *De Sacramentis*, II, n. 181.

[101] Canon 995, § 2.

[102] S. C. de Religiosis, instr. "*Quantum religiones*," 1 dec. 1931, n. 12—*AAS*, XXIV (1932), 78.

[103] Coronata, *De Sacramentis*, II, n. 181; Cappello, *De Sacra Ordinatione*, n. 344. Cf. S. C. C., *Nullius*, 16 ian. 1595, in S. C. C., *Elboren.*, 2 et 23 aug. 1721, ad 3—*Thesaurus Resolutionum Sacrae Congregationis Concilii* (167 vols., Romae, 1718-1908), II, 65-69 (hereafter cited *Thesaurus SCC*).

[104] Canon 995, § 1.

[105] Canon 1001, § 4.

fore his first profession and again before promotion to the subdiaconate have been made according to the norms of the Instruction *Quantum religiones*.[106]

Some authors require that the phrase *deque aliis iure requisitis* of canon 995, § 1, is to be understood as requiring a specific enumeration of the requirements which have actually been met. Thus Goyeneche requires data be given on confirmation, the candidate's character, his age, his possession of the necessary knowledge, his reception of the preceding order, the observance of the interstices, and, if major orders are to be received, the existence of a canonical title.[107] Schaefer lists as matters to be inserted in the dimissorial letters, in addition to the items stipulated in canon 995, § 1, the last order received by the candidate, a statement about the candidate's character, his age, his freedom from irregularities and impediments, and the performance by him of the spiritual exercises.[108] As elements to be noted in the dimissorial letters, Coronata adds to the items in canon 995, § 1, the testimony of the candidate's baptism and confirmation or of the last order received by him, his possession of good moral qualities, his freedom from impediments, and the fulfillment of the requisite of the spiritual retreat.[109] The requirements demanded by these authors are illustrative of the interpretation given to the phrase by other commentators.

In practice, since printed forms are frequently used, such listings will conveniently serve to recall to the superior and the minister the various demands of canon law affecting candidates for ordination. For before the superior prepares the letters, he must comply with the several requirements, whether or not an exhaustive listing is given in the printed forms of dimissorial letters. However, such an enumeration does not seem to be necessary specifically in order that the letters be described as complete. For the very granting of the dimissorial letters is in itself an attestation that the candidate is a fit subject for orders, a state-

---

106 *Supra*, pp. 34-38.

107 "Consultationes"—*CpR*, III (1922), 264.

108 *De Religiosis*, n. 454.

109 *De Sacramentis*, II, n. 181.

ment which cannot be made if some deficiency still needs to be satisfied.[110] Hence it seems that it is sufficient for the superior to indicate only in a general manner that the requirements of the law have been met, so that a detailed enumeration of these requirements need not be set down in the dimissorials.[111]

The dimissorial letters are to be directed to the bishop who has the right to receive them, even though he will permit another to ordain in his stead. Thus the letters should not be addressed to the auxiliary bishop of the diocese, even though it is known that he will perform the ceremony, but to the residential bishop of the diocese.[112] The practice is to add to this designation an alternate provision which allows the candidate to be promoted by any bishop in communion with the Holy See.[113]

Since dimissorial letters are official documents, they should be prepared in a manner which will reveal and preserve their authenticity. Although the standard portion may be printed or typewritten, the signature of the superior should be handwritten, and his seal attached or embossed, so that any change or mutilation which might occur may be readily detected.[114]

Dimissorial letters can be recalled or limited either by the superior or by his successor, but they continue in force until this revocation has been signified in some way, either to the candidate or to the bishop to whom they were addressed.[115] The letters remain valid even after the grantor surrenders his office or otherwise loses his right to prepare further letters.[116]

---

[110] Canon 995, § 1, uses the expression *suis litteris dimissoriis* without the preposition *in*. It appears to be the better interpretation, then, to say that the superior testifies to the fulfillment of the various requisites for ordination *by means of* his dimissorial letters rather than *in* his dimissorial letters.

[111] Cf. Gallagher, *The Examination of the Qualities of the Ordinand*, pp. 116-117.

[112] Gasparri, *De Sacra Ordinatione*, n. 878; Many, *De Sacra Ordinatione*, n. 63; Regatillo, *Ius Sacramentarium*, II, n. 59.

[113] Cf. Beste, *Introductio*, p. 520.

[114] Cf. Gasparri, *De Sacra Ordinatione*, n. 740.

[115] Cappello, *De Sacra Ordinatione*, n 345.

[116] Canon 963.

CHAPTER IV

THE MINISTER OF ORDINATION

The ordinary minister of sacred ordination is a consecrated bishop; the extraordinary minister is one who has received either by law or by a special indult of the Holy See the power of conferring some orders, even though he may lack episcopal consecration.[1] There is no need at this juncture to undertake a study of the theological basis upon which this power is based, since the Code, for all practical purposes, determines the persons who can ordain and the conditions for a valid and licit ordination.

A consecrated bishop, if he observes the proper matter and form and with the proper intention ordains a suitable subject, validly confers orders.[2] The extraordinary ministers, however, are further limited by conditions as to the orders they can confer, the subjects they can ordain, and the place of ordination. Unless these conditions are observed, the ordination may be invalid. By common law, cardinals,[3] vicars and prefects apostolic,[4] abbots and prelates *nullius,*[5] and regular abbots *de regimine*[6] can confer tonsure and minor orders.

Cardinals who have been ordained to the priesthood[7] can, after their promotion in the Consistory, confer tonsure and minor orders on any candidate, provided that the latter has dimissorial letters from his proper Ordinary.[8] If the ordination were performed without dimissorial letters, it appears that the promotion would be invalid.[9]

---

[1] Canon 951.

[2] Conc. Trident., sess. XXIII, *de ordine,* c. 4, can. 7; Gasparri, *De Sacra Ordinatione,* n. 774; Many, *De Sacra Ordinatione,* n. 27.

[3] Canon 239, § 1, 22°.

[4] Canons 294, § 2; 957, § 2.

[5] Canons 323, § 2; 957, § 2.

[6] Canon 964, 1°.

[7] Cf. canon 232, § 1.

[8] Canon 239, § 1, 22°.

[9] Hynes, *The Privileges of Cardinals,* The Catholic University of America Canon Law Studies, n. 217 (Washington, D. C.: The Catholic University of America Press, 1945), p. 65; Sipos, *Enchiridion Iuris Canonici,* p. 453, footnote 9. Cf. Wernz-Vidal, *Ius Canonicum,* I, n. 162, footnote 144.

Vicars and prefects apostolic, and abbots and prelates *nullius* can likewise confer tonsure and minor orders, but only within their own territory, during their term of assignment, and, in addition to their subjects, on such as have requisite dimissorial letters. An ordination contrary to these limitations is invalid.[10] This right is acquired from the time the prelate takes possession of his office.[11] An abbot *nullius,* even though he may be required to receive the abbatial blessing, seems capable of ordaining even before this blessing is received.[12] The priesthood is presupposed for these offices.[13]

Since regular abbots *de regimine* can confer tonsure and minor orders in their capacity as religious superiors, the discussion of their power to ordain is taken up at that point.[14]

If any of the extraordinary ministers is also a consecrated bishop, he is not limited to the conditions listed for the validity of the ordination. Besides these ministers mentioned in the Code, the Holy See can empower others to ordain. The limits and conditions of the grant must be examined in each case before one can determine the extent of the minister's competency.

ARTICLE I. THE SUPERIOR AS MINISTER

A. *A General Minister of Orders*

Those who can issue dimissorial letters for the promotion to orders can themselves confer these orders if they possess the necessary power to ordain.[15] The legislator explicitly indicates that the power to issue dimissorial letters is but another expression of the right to ordain. While there can be some doubt about the application of this canon to religious, since it seems to be associated with the preceding canons which deal with the ordi-

[10] Canon 957, § 2.

[11] Canon 293, § 2 with 311; 322, § 1.

[12] Benko, *The Abbot Nullius,* The Catholic University of America Canon Law Studies, n. 173 (Washington, D. C.: The Catholic University of America Press, 1943), p. 83.

[13] Canon 118 with 154.

[14] *Infra,* pp. 68 ff.

[15] Canon 959.

nation of seculars,[16] nevertheless the general wording of the canon, the lack of historical precedents to limit the interpretation, and the support given by prominent canonists[17] tends to favor the interpretation that a religious superior, if he enjoys the power to ordain, may himself confer orders on those of his subjects for whom he can issue dimissorial letters, without obtaining permission from the proper bishop.

It cannot be objected that such an interpretation violates the right of the diocesan bishop. Neither the Clementine decree[18] nor canon 965 require that the candidate be ordained by the bishop of the diocese. The law restricts the superior only in the choice of persons to whom the dimissorial letters may be addressed. Since no letters are required when the superior himself ordains, there is no violation of the diocesan bishop's right to receive them.

The minister must be the one and the same person who can issue dimissorial letters for the ordination. It is not sufficient that the minister be a member of the institute or even another superior, though without jurisdiction over the candidate, in the same institute, for in neither case would there exist the necessary concurrence of the power and the right to ordain. A Cardinal Protector does not by common law enjoy jurisdiction in the religious institute.[19] Unless the approved constitutions provide otherwise, he can neither issue dimissorial letters on behalf of the members nor ordain them in his own right.

While the permission of the diocesan bishop is not needed for a religious superior to ordain his own subjects, the consent of the local ordinary may be required if pontifical insignia are used for

[16] Goyeneche, "Consultationes"—*CpR,* V (1924), 164-165. Prümmer (*Manuale Iuris Canonici,* Q. 318, 5) allows the Superior to ordain only if he occupies also the position of a local Ordinary. Many (*De Sacra Ordinatione,* n. 161, 3) before the Code allowed it only if the institute had the privilege to approach any Bishop for orders.

[17] Cappello, *De Sacra Ordinatione,* n. 346; Coronata, *De Sacramentis,* II, n. 37; Schaefer, *De Religiosis,* n. 460; Wernz-Vidal, *Ius Canonicum,* IV, i, n. 197; (Anonymous) "De Ordinatione a Proprio Superiore Religioso"—*Periodica,* XII (1924), (163)-(164). Gasparri (*De Sacra Ordinatione,* n. 918) maintained this opinion already before the Code.

[18] S. C. C., decr. 15 mart. 1596—*Fontes,* n. 2294.

[19] Canon 499, § 2.

the ordination. This matter is discussed later in reference to the place of ordination.[20]

B. *The Regular Abbot de regimine*

In the Eastern Church, longer than in the West, it was considered proper for all the faithful to attend and participate in the celebration of the canonical hours. Like other members of the laity, the monks frequented a neighboring church and there joined in the ceremonies. As monastic churches became established, the monks continued to solemnize the divine praises. Even though the office of lector had become the order of lector, the monks, though not ordained, continued to perform the duties proper to the former office.[21] This usurpation by monks of functions proper to a clerical order gradually brought about the acceptance of monastic profession as the equivalent of minor orders.[22] The legislation in the Rule of St. Benedict adds support to this view. Although the seniority of the monks and their precedence in the community was ordinarily dependent on the time they came to the monastery,[23] an ordained priest, on acceptance into the monastery, could be ranked after the abbot, while a cleric was placed in a middle position.[24] Since most of the monks were laymen, reverence for the priesthood placed such a priest-monk ahead of the usual position he would normally have occupied, so that he ranked immediately after the abbot. But a cleric, being superior to a layman, should also have ranked ahead of the lay community, and not have been stationed in a middle position as among equals. Further, while the Rule provides for the ordination of priests and deacons, no mention is made of the lower orders.[25] These

---

[20] *Infra*, pp. 119 ff.

[21] Kozman, *Textes Legislatifs touchant le Cenobitisme Egyptien*, pp. 47-50; *Regula*, c. IX-XI.

[22] Thomassinus, *Vetus et Nova Ecclesiae Disciplina* (10 vols., Magontiaci, 1787), Pars I, lib. iii, c. xxxvi, n. 16; Molitor, *Religiosi Iuris Capita Selecta* (Romae, 1909), n. 222.

[23] *Regula*, c. LXIII.

[24] *Regula*, c. LX.

[25] *Regula*, c. LXII.

provisions can be conveniently explained if monastic profession was considered as the equivalent of ordination to minor orders.

A letter of Pope Gregory the Great (590-604) gave a candidate the alternative of becoming a monk or a subdeacon as a prerequisite for higher orders.[26]

It was precisely this usurpation of duties proper to the order of lector by those who had not been ordained to that rank that prompted the II Council of Nicaea (787) to provide a canonical remedy for the abuse by empowering monastic superiors to confer the order of lector in their own monasteries, provided the superior had received the imposition of hands and was a priest.[27] Balsamon (1140-ca. 1195) explained that the Council granted the power of ordination to the monastic superiors because the nature of the monastic life, especially in the East, made it inconvenient for monks to come to the cities for ordination by the bishop, who, on the other hand, was to be spared a journey to the country.[28] The canon was accepted into Gratian's *Decree*, and formed the legal basis of the abbatial power to ordain.[29]

The Code empowers regular abbots *de regimine* to confer tonsure and minor orders on their subjects who have made at least simple profession, provided that the abbot has legitimately received the abbatial blessing and is a priest. Beyond these limits the ordination is invalid, unless the abbot is a consecrated bishop. All contrary privileges are revoked.[30]

1. Qualities Required in the Minister

The power to ordain was conferred, by the II Council of Nicaea, on the *hegumenus*, one of several titles applied to religious superiors, but without the connotation of a dignity.[31] According to

---

[26] *Ad Passivum—Epistolae*, XII, 4; Jaffé, n. 1855.

[27] Canon 14—Mansi, XIII, 434.

[28] *Commentarius in XIV canone VII Synodi—PG*, CXXXVII, 959-960.

[29] C. 1, D. LXIX.

[30] Canon 964, 1°.

[31] Coussa, *Epitome Iuris Orientalis*, II, 23, footnote 53; Morinus, *Commentarius de Sacris Eccleasiae Ordinationibus* (Parisiis, 1655), Pars II, p. 247; De Meester, *De Monachico Statu iuxta Disciplinam Byzantinam*, Codificazione Canonica Orientale, *Fonti*, Serie II, Fascicolo X (Civitate Vaticana: Typis Polyglottis Vaticanis, 1942), pp. 197-199.

the Latin version, the minister was an *abbas,* an abbot. This term was used in designation of the superior who ruled a monastic community.[82] At the time the Nicaean canon was introduced into the Western Church, the monastic form of the religious life predominated. It was during that period, too, that abbots began to receive the privilege of using the pontifical insignia.[83] Hence, with the rise of non-monastic religious institutes, whose superiors were not styled abbots, the power to ordain was not accorded to them.[84] Thus the superiors in the Mendicant orders[85] and non-abbatial monastic superiors, such as conventual priors, could not ordain.

At the present time the term *abbot* not only indicates a religious superior but also implies a dignity.[86] The legislator has seen fit to restrict the power of ordaining to regular abbots *de regimine.* A Regular abbot is one that belongs to a religious order.[87] This is in contrast with secular abbots, who are not members of a religious order, but possess the title and benefice of an extinct monastic foundation,[88] and commendatory abbots, who formerly re-

[82] Cf. *Regula,* c. II.

[83] Cf. Oesterle, *Praelectiones Iuris Canonici* (manuscripti instar), I (Romae: Collegio S. Anselmi, 1931), pp. 349-353; Chamard, "Les Abbés au Moyen Age"—*Revue des Questions Historiques* (Paris, 1866-), XXXVIII (1885), 82-108.

[84] Cf. Van Espen, *Jus Ecclesiasticum Universum* (10 vols., Venetiis, 1769), Lib. I, tit. 31, n. 17.

[85] Pope Clement V (1305-1314) allowed priests of the Order of Friars Minor to confer tonsure and minor orders on candidates of their own institute. The use of the faculty was limited to those engaged in missionary work among the dissidents of Eastern Europe, and could be used only when a Catholic bishop was unavailable. Const. *"Cum hora nona,"* 21 iul. 1307—Waddingus, *Annales Minorum* (ed. nova, 25 vols., Ad Claras Aquas, 1931-1934), VI, 111.

[86] Gómez, "De Abbatum Potestate Tonsuram Minoresque Ordines Conferendi"—*CpR,* IX (1928), 439.

[87] Canon 488, 7°. Canons Regular who have an abbot as a superior are the Premonstratensians of St. Norbert, the Lateran Canons of the Most Holy Savior, and the Augustinian Canons of the Great St. Bernard, whose prior receives the abbatial blessing. Monks ruled by abbots are the Benedictines, the Cistercians of both observances, the Vallumbrosians, and the Silvestrines.

[88] Only by privilege can secular abbots ordain. Cf. S. C. C., *Lucana,* 14 apr., 1 sept., 17 nov. 1725—*Thesaurus SCC,* III, 155-157, 214-217, 230-234, 293-296. S. C. Ep. et Reg., *Tarvisina,* 8 apr. 1859—*Fontes,* n. 1978. Benedictus

ceived the benefice of a flourishing abbey, but remained without any ruling power.[39] The Regular abbot must also be *de regimine*, that is, actually engaged in the government of a monastery *sui iuris* as its abbot. This distinguishes him from titular abbots, who, even though they may belong to an order, hold the title of an extinct abbey without any rights or subjects,[40] and from abbots who have ceased from office, as by resignation.[41] An abbot to whom a coadjutor is given does not thereby lose the faculty for ordaining. The powers of the coadjutor must be determined from his letters of assignment.[42]

The Abbot Primate cannot, by common law, ordain others than of the abbey of St. Anselm.[43] In virtue of a special faculty, however, he can during his term of office confer tonsure and minor orders on the student members of the College attached to that abbey, provided that the candidates have dimissorial letters from their own abbot.[44]

The superiors of monastic congregations likewise do not have from the Code any faculty to ordain. The Holy See had, already

---

XIV, *De Synodo Dioecesana*, lib. II, cap. 11, n. 10. The Superior of the canons of the church at Guadelupe in Mexico enjoys such a dignity.

[39] Cf. canon 1412, 5°. Commendatory abbots were not only forbidden to ordain, but also in any way to interfere in the community. Cf. S. C. C., *Neapolitana*, 1 dec. 1668—Pallottini, s.v. *Sacramentum Ordinis*, II, n. 28; S. C. C., *Caputaquen.*, 17 dec. 1712—Pallottini, s.v. *Sacramentum Ordinis*, II, n. 24; S. C. Ep. et Reg., *Messanen.*, 20 sept. 1697—Bizzarri, *Collectanea in Usum Secretariae Sacrae Congregationis Episcoporum et Regularium* (Romae, 1885), p. 282 (hereafter cited Bizzarri).

[40] S. C. S. Off., 15 iul. 1903—*Fontes*, n. 1268. Ordinarily they do not receive the abbatial blessing nor do they have the use of pontifical insignia. Cf. S. R. C., dubiorum, 14 dec. 1904—*Decreta Authentica Congregationis Sacrorum Rituum* (5 vols. et 2 Appendices, Romae, 1898-1927), n. 4148 (hereafter cited *Decr. Auth.*).

[41] S. C. C., *Congregationis Olivetanae*, 29 nov. 1788—*Fontes*, n. 3861.

[42] Augustine, *Commentary*, IV, 435; Beste, *Introductio*, p. 517.

[43] Leo XIII, litt. ap. "*Summum semper*," 12 iul. 1893—*Fontes*, n. 619; S. C. et Reg., decr. 16 sept. 1893—*Fontes*, n. 2022.

[44] S. C. de Religiosis, decr. 28 febr. 1920—*Annales OSB*, XXVIII-XXXIV (1920-1926), 87-88. The faculty had originally been granted by Pope Pius X (1903-1914), though no mention was made of tonsure. Cf. rescr. 20 maii 1908—*Annales OSB*, XI-XVI (1903-1908), 22-23.

before the Code, ruled that an abbot general of the Silvestrines did not have the power to ordain members of the order,[45] but admitted as valid, though illicit, an ordination performed by an abbot upon a candidate over whom he had cumulative power with the ordinand's abbot, at whose instance the ordination was performed.[46] The superiors of monastic congregations received the authority to ordain members of their congregation who presented dimissorial letters from their own abbot in the same grant made to the Abbot Primate, but their faculty was not renewed after the Code.[47] Unless the constitutions of the particular monastic congregation state otherwise, the superiors of monastic congregations do not enjoy the power to ordain members of their congregation.

Other superiors in monastic congregations, such as the vicar general[48] and the visitators, also are devoid of the right to ordain members of the congregation in virtue of their office.[49]

The powers of an abbot appointed apostolic administrator of another abbey by the Holy See would have to be determined in each case from the letters of his appointment.

Conventual priors, even though they are major superiors, cannot make use of the faculty primarily because they are not abbots. Should they be titular abbots and rule a priory, they cannot validly ordain members of that community.[50]

Further, the regular abbot *de regimine,* in order to enjoy the power to ordain, must be a priest. At the time of the II Council of Nicaea (787) not all monastic superiors were priests.[51] Although the priesthood was not necessary for the office of superior, it was

---

[45] S. C. C., dubium 26 febr. 1622—Pallottini, s.v. *Sacramentum Ordinis,* III, n. 70.

[46] S. C. C., *Anglonen.,* 15 maii 1802—*Thesaurus SCC,* LXVIII, 94-95; Pallottini, s.v. *Sacramentum Ordinis,* III, n. 65.

[47] *Supra,* p. 71.

[48] S. C. C., *Nullius,* 5 apr. 1636—Pallottini, s.v. *Abbas,* III, n. 11.

[49] Visitators were judged as not the equivalent of the abbot *de regimine* in so far as the election of the Abbot Primate was concerned. Cf. S. C. de Religiosis, dubium 12 febr. 1913—*Annales OSB,* XXI (1913), 14-15.

[50] S. C. S. Off., 15 iul. 1903—*Fontes,* n. 1268.

[51] Cf. canon 19—Mansi, XIII, 434.

considered a necessary condition for the power to ordain.[52] Hence it was necessary to explicitly specify that the superior be an ordained priest.

In the Western Church, too, not all abbots were ordained to the priesthood, as is apparent from legislation of several councils. Thus the monastic Chapter of Aachen (817) allowed abbots who were not priests to give the blessing to the reader.[53] At the Council of Rome (853) abbots were urged to become priests that they might curb and remove the sins of their subjects.[54] The Council of Poitiers (1078) required all abbots to become priests or else lose their prelacy.[55] The priesthood as a condition for enjoying the faculty of ordination was explicitly mentioned in the original version of the Nicaean canon and in the subsequent restatements of it.[56] The Code likewise makes explicit mention of the order of priesthood in the abbot as a necessary condition for the validity of the ordination.[57] The rite of the abbatial blessing presupposes that the abbot who is to be blessed is a priest, for during the ceremony he is garbed in sacerdotal vestments.[58]

This requirement of the abbatial blessing is the third quality required in an abbot if he is to enjoy the faculty of ordaining. Although some confusion arises in determining exactly what was meant by the "imposition of hands" as required by the Nicaean canon,[59] since the expression was used for the purpose of describing both the abbatial blessing and the ordination of the lectors,

---

[52] Balsamon, *Commentarius in XIV canone VII Synodi—PG,* CXXXVII, 961-962.

[53] Canon 62—Mansi, XVIIA, 586. This did not imply that they could ordain lectors, but rather that they could give the blessing to the lector before he read in church. Cf. Gonzales-Tellez, *Commentaria Perpetua in Singulos Textus Quinque Librorum Decretalium Gregorii IX* (5 vols., Venetiis, 1699), Lib. I, tit. 14, n. 11. Cf. also *Regula,* c. IX, XI, LX; Molitor, *Religiosi Iuris Capita Selecta,* nn. 218, 222, 352.

[54] Canon 27—Mansi, XIV, 1007.

[55] Canon 7—Mansi, XX, 498.

[56] C. 1, D. LXIX; c. 11, *de aetate et qualitate et ordine praeficiendorum,* I, 14; c. 3, *de privilegiis,* V, 7, in VI°.

[57] Canon 964, 1°.

[58] Pontificale Rom., *De benedictione abbatis auctoritate apostolica.*

[59] Cf. Molitor, *Religiosi Iuris Capita Selecta,* n. 361-362.

it seems quite clear that this described a rite different from sacerdotal ordination and the equivalent of the present abbatial blessing.[60]

Until 1725, a newly elected abbot was not bound by the common law to receive the abbatial blessing. Yet, until he had received it, he could not perform actions permitted to a blessed abbot, such as ordaining.[61] He could ordain his Regular subjects if he had received the abbatial blessing.[62]

In three cases, however, the abbot could ordain even though he had not received the abbatial blessing. If the bishop thrice refused to confer the blessing, abbots were permitted the full abbatial power without a blessing. Pope Alexander III (1159-1181) originally allowed this to the Cistercian abbots, but the principle was adopted as common law.[63] Yet even in this case the abbatial prerogatives could not be used until the election of the abbot had been confirmed.[64] A second exception to the necessity of a blessing was verified if by privilege the abbot was excused from seeking a blessing and yet was allowed the full use of the abbatial powers as if he had been blessed.[65] A third exception was introduced by

[60] Morinus (*Commentarius de Sacris Ecclesiae Ordinationibus,* Pars II, pp. 72, 82, 96, 103, 118) furnishes several formulae used for this rite in the East, all of which contain an imposition of the hands. The abbatial blessing as given in the *Pontificale,* though much more elaborate than the Eastern blessings, also contains an imposition of the hands over the abbot being blessed. Cf. tit. *De benedictione abbatis auctoritate apostolica.* Cf. De Meester, *De Monachico Statu iuxta Disciplinam Byzantinam,* pp. 237-240.

[61] *Glossa ordinaria* ad c. 11, X, *de aetate et qualitate et ordine praeficiendorum,* I, 14, s.v. *abbati;* S. C. C., *Posnanien.,* 16 apr. 1639—Pallottini, s.v. *Abbas,* II, n. 40-41; S. C. C., *Calaritana,* 13 febr. 1639—*Fontes,* n. 2599; S. C. C., *Panormitana,* 16 mart. 1647, ad I1—Pallottini, s.v. *Abbas,* III, n. 124.

[62] S. C. C., *Catanien.,* 15 febr. 1642—*Fontes,* n. 2631; S. C. C., *Leodien.,* 14 mart. 1648—*Fontes,* n. 2680.

[63] C. 1, X, *de supplenda negligentia praelatorum,* I, 10; Jaffé, n. 11632.

[64] *Glossa ordinaria* ad c. 1, X, *de supplenda negligentia praelatorum,* I, 10, s.v. *substitutos.* In virtue of a further privilege of Pope Clement IV (1265-1268), the election of Cistercian abbots was considered as approved as soon as it had taken place, without further recourse to the Holy See. Cf. Const. *"Parvus fons,"* 9 iun. 1265—*Bull. Rom. Taur.,* III, 732; Potthast, n. 19185.

[65] S. C. C., dubium 20 oct. 1579—Pallottini, s.v. *Abbas,* III, n. 60; S. C. C., *Portugalien.,* 2 apr. 1591—*Fontes,* n. 2227; S. C. C., *Tullen.,* 21 mart. 1596, ad 7—*Fontes,* n. 2295; S. C. C., *Panormitana,* 16 mart. 1647, ad 1—*Fontes,*

Pope Benedict XIII (1724-1730). He required that thenceforth all abbots should present themselves to the local bishop or the metropolitan within a year of their election to obtain the abbatial blessing, unless they enjoyed a contrary privilege. During this year, however, the newly chosen abbot was permitted to exercise all the functions proper to a blessed abbot.[66]

By the law of the Code, all Regular abbots *de regimine* must receive the abbatial blessing within three months of their election from the bishop of the diocese in whose territory the monastery is located.[67] No provision is made in the Code for cases in which the bishop refuses to confer the blessing, is absent, or otherwise impeded, or when the see is vacant. In such cases the provisions of the pre-Code discipline no longer apply,[68] and recourse must be had to the Holy See.[69] Until the abbot has received the blessing, he cannot validly ordain.

Although the abbatial blessing is to be received at the hands of the diocesan bishop, the latter may not proceed until he has received from the Holy See a mandate to confer the blessing.[70] If,

---

n. 2671. Such a privilege had been granted by Pope Eugene IV (1431-1447) to the abbots of the Congregation of St. Justina (Cassinese)—Const. *"Regularem vitam,"* 30 iun. 1436—*Bull. Rom. Taur.*, V, 25-26. Pope Julius II (1503-1513) allowed a similar privilege to the Olivetans—Const. *"Etsi ad universos,"* 31 maii 1507, § 17—Bull. Rom. Taur., V, 447.

[66] Const. *"Commissi Nobis,"* 6 maii 1725—*Fontes*, n. 287.

[67] Canon 625. Although privileges excusing abbots from receiving the blessing are not revoked by canon 625, the blessing is necessary for the valid conferral of orders. Beste, *Introductio*, p. 428; *contra* Augustine, *Commentary*, III, 355.

[68] Canon 6, 6°.

[69] Augustine, *Commentary*, III, 355. Pope Benedict XV (1914-1922) granted Benedictine abbots the concession whereby they might receive the abbatial blessing from any bishop in communion with the Holy See as often as the diocesan see was vacant, and, if it was so stated in writing, also when the diocesan bishop was legitimately impeded or gave his consent.—Litt. ap. *"Pro benedictione,"* 19 iun. 1921—*AAS*, XIII (1921), 416-417.

[70] Pontificale Rom., tit. *De benedictione abbatis auctoritate apostolica.* Abbots belonging to the Benedictine Confederation make use of a mandate granted *semel pro semper* by Pope Benedict XV. Cf. litt. ap. *"Pro benedictione,"* 19 iun. 1921—*AAS*, XIII (1921), 416-417.

by special permission of the Holy See, the abbatial blessing is conferred by an abbot instead of by a bishop, the ordinations performed by an abbot so blessed cannot be questioned on the charge that he had not been lawfully blessed.[71] Unlike the episcopal consecration which it so closely resembles, the abbatial blessing does not imprint a character, which is the radical source of the bishop's power to ordain.[72] It is rather a condition imposed by the legislator for the use of the faculty of ordaining by an extraordinary minister.

2. The Subject of Ordination

The Code specifically restricts the power of ordination enjoyed by an abbot *de regimine* to those who are his subjects at least by simple profession. An ordination performed on a candidate who is not such a subject is invalid, unless the abbot is a consecrated bishop.[73] The original canon of the II Council of Nicaea (787) did not contain such a restriction; but it seems to have been understood that the faculty would be used only on behalf of subjects of the superior, since the use of the power to ordain was restricted to the minister's own monastery.[74] In the Eastern Church this posed no problem, since each superior could have jurisdiction in only one monastery.[75] For all practical purposes, his power was limited to members of the community he ruled.

In the Western Church, too, the abbot could ordain only in his own monastery,[76] but, if invited, he could ordain the monks of another monastery[77] just as a bishop could ordain the subjects of another bishop.[78] Although laymen who received tonsure at the

[71] S. C. C., *Vratislavien.*, 12 febr. 1724—*Fontes*, n. 3274. In modern times a similar grant has been made to the Hungarian Congregation of Benedictines, whose archabbot can bless newly elected abbots of the Congregation. Cf. Benedictus XV, breve ap. *"Curavit,"* 13 dec. 1921—*AAS*, XIV (1922), 34.

[72] Molitor, *Religiosi Iuris Capita Selecta*, n. 373.

[73] Canon 964, 1°.

[74] Balsamon, Zonaras, Aristenes, *Commentarius in XIV canone VII Synodi* —*PG*, CXXXVII, 961-962.

[75] Cf. Photius, *Nomocanon*, Tit. I, c. 20—*PG*, CIV, 1001-1002.

[76] *Glossa ordinaria* ad c. 1, D. LXIX, s.v. *tonsura vero*.

[77] *Glossa ordinaria* ad c. 1, D. LXIX, s.v. *monasterio*.

[78] The glossators referred to the letter of Pope Urban II (1088-1099) to the Archbishop of Lyons. C. 10, C. IX, q. 2; Jaffé, n. 5723.

hands of an abbot were validly promoted,[79] Pope Alexander IV (1254-1261) restricted abbots in the conferring of orders to members of the monastery subject to them, to those who came to join the monastery, and to those over whom the abbot exercised quasi-episcopal power.[80] Nevertheless, non-subjects could be validly ordained if the abbot received that power by indult,[81] or, as some of the texts that were used in the compiling of the *Liber Sextus* indicate, if the practice of ordaining non-subjects existed as a custom which was duly accompanied with the factor of legal prescription.[82]

The Council of Trent (1545-1563) did not re-define the abbatial power of conferring orders, but limited its use to the abbot's Regular subjects.[83] Considerable controversy arose on the point whether the ordinations performed by abbots *de regimine* contrary to the restriction of the Council of Trent were invalid, or, though valid, still illicit. The decisions of the Sacred Congregations upheld the right of the abbot to ordain his own Regular subjects. As to orders conferred by him on other Regulars and seculars, the ordinations were first held to be licit if performed with the permission of the candidate's ordinary, then held to be illicit, and finally held to be invalid. Canonists differed on the question. But inasmuch as each could cite decisions of the Sacred Congregations favorable to his view, the presented view naturally received continued support.

The attitude that the Council of Trent sought only to preserve for the bishop his right to ordain candidates from his diocese underlies an early decision which permitted abbots, if they were priests and had received the blessing, to ordain seculars subject to the bishop, provided that the candidate had proper dimissorial letters. However, no general permission could be given to an abbot for such ordinations, but a special permission was required for each ordination. Regulars who were not his subjects could

---

[79] C. 11, X, *de aetate et qualitate et ordine praeficiendorum,* I, 14.
[80] C. 3, *de privilegiis,* V, 7, in VI°; Potthast, n. 18116.
[81] *Glossa ordinaria* ad c. 3, *de privilegiis,* V, 7, in VI°, s.v. *indulto.*
[82] Cf. Friedberg's notes to c. 3, *de privilegiis,* V, 7, in VI°.
[83] Conc. Trident., sess. XXIII, *de ref.,* c. 10.

also be ordained by an abbot, provided that they presented dimissorial letters from their ordinaries and also the special permission through which the bishop had waived his right to ordain.[84]

Schmalzgrueber (1663-1735), who defended this opinion, offered the following explanation: The restriction imposed by the Council of Trent on the abbot's power to ordain affected only that faculty which was derived from the common law or from an indult, and not also that which could arise from the permission or delegation of a bishop. While the Council restricted the abbatial power in favor of the bishop, this prerogative was not to become a burden on the bishop. Hence he could authorize an abbot to ordain secular subjects on his behalf.[85]

Other decisions of the Holy See rebuked abbots for ordaining candidates who were not their subjects, since thus the right of the diocesan Bishop was violated.[86]

In 1642 Pope Urban VIII (1623-1644) ruled, through the Sacred Congregation of the Council, that thenceforth abbots were forbidden to ordain non-subjects, and other prelates were forbidden to direct dimissorial letters to them for the ordination of such candidates. Through any violation of this rule both the grantor of the letters and the ordaining abbot were *ipso iure* suspended from conferring orders.[87] Subsequent decisions insisted on the observance of the policy instituted by Pope Urban VIII.[88]

The Congregation of Sacred Rites issued an instruction on the use of pontifical insignia by abbots and minor prelates. Once again abbots were reminded that they were forbidden to exercise their prerogatives outside of places or in relation to persons not

---

[84] S. C. C., *Bononien.*, 2 iul. 1572 in S. C. C., *Brixien.*, 12 dec. 1733, ad VI-VIII—*Thesaurus SCC*, VI, 202. Cf. S. C. C., *Parmen.*, mensis aug. 1586—Pallottini, s.v. *Abbas*, III, n. 20-21.

[85] *Jus Ecclesiasticum Universum* (5 vols. in 12, Romae, 1843-1845), Lib. I, tit. xi, n. 32.

[86] S. C. C., *Cremonen.*, 13 iun. 1591—Pallottini, s.v. *Abbas*, III, n. 120; S. C. C., *Theatina*, 26 sept. 1615, ad I—Pallottini, s.v. *Abbas*, III, n. 139, 163.

[87] S. C. C., *Catanien.*, 15 febr. 1642—*Fontes*, n. 2631.

[88] S. C. C., *Portugalliae*, 7 aug. 1649, ad 2—*Fontes*, n. 2698; S. C. C., *Lamacen.*, 13 aug. 1707, 26 ian. 1709, ad 2, 16 dec. 1713, ad 1—*Fontes*, n. 3057, 3073, 3129.

subject to them. The conferring of minor orders was specifically indicated as one of the restricted functions.[89]

By far the more serious problem was the validity of an ordination performed by an abbot on a candidate who was not his subject. At the instance of Pope Clement VIII (1592-1605), precisely this question, namely, whether abbots who enjoyed the faculty to ordain their Regular subjects could also with proper dimissorial letters ordain other candidates, was submitted to the Rota. This tribunal decided that abbots could not confer orders on persons other than the Regulars who were subject to them, since the faculty whereby abbots ordained was revoked except in regard to their Regular subjects.[90] In 1642, when Pope Urban VIII prohibited abbots to ordain non-subjects, he convalidated the orders which had been improperly conferred.[91]

In the cases presented before the year 1774 the Sacred Congregation of the Council decided that an ordination performed by an abbot who enjoyed the faculty of conferring orders was a valid promotion, but the exercise of an act that was illicit.[92] In that year another case was presented. In it the Sacred Congregation again upheld the validity of tonsure and minor orders conferred by an abbot on a candidate who was not his subject. The decision seems to have been based on the canonical teaching of Fagnanus, who was quoted in the notes of the case.[93]

Fagnanus (1598-1678) held that the abbatial power to ordain was a combination of the power of orders and of the power of jurisdiction. The abbatial blessing, while not essential for an abbot to be an abbot, was necessary for the conferring of orders, since the power to ordain did not derive from the office of abbot. This

[89] S. R. C., decr. 27 sept. 1659, n. 19—*Decr. Auth.*, n. 1131; *Fontes*, n. 5518.

[90] S. R. R., *Decisio 985 coram Seraphino* in S. C. C., *Collen.*, 24 ian. 1795—*Thesaurus SCC*, LXIV, 6.

[91] S. C. C., *Catanien.*, 15 febr. 1642—*Fontes*, n. 2631.

[92] S. C. C., *Panormitana*, 16 mart. 1647, ad II—Pallottini, s.v. *Abbas*, III, n. 124; S. C. C., *Conimbricen.*, 26 iun. 1655, ad 1—*Fontes*, n. 2743; S. C. C., dubium 11 maii 1658—Pallottini, s.v. *Abbas*, III, n. 192; S. C. C., *Brixien.*, 28 nov. 12 dec. 1733, ad VI-VIII—*Fontes*, n. 3411.

[93] S. C. C., *Hispalen. Ordinum*, 18 sept. 1773, 12 mart. 1774—*Thesaurus SCC*, XLII, 166-173; XLIII, 38-40.

blessing could be omitted only under the conditions accepted in law.[94] It was in the reception of his blessing that the abbot, by a concession of the Church, received the authority to confer orders.[95] But in the privilege or commission to ordain there were contained two elements, viz., the basic power of ordination and the jurisdiction to use this power, though the use was restricted to specified persons. However, this limitation of jurisdiction did not in any way limit the extent of the power to ordain. Since the Council of Trent had not taken away the basic power of ordaining persons other than his regular subjects, but simply forbade such to be ordained by him, the abbot still retained the power to ordain persons other than those specified by the Council.[96]

In 1795, the Sacred Congregation of the Council reviewed the case of a secular student who had been ordained by an abbot after dimissorial letters were furnished by the candidate's bishop. After reviewing several past decisions of the Holy See and delving into the doctrines of the leading canonists, the Sacred Congregation ruled that the ordination was invalid and was to be repeated secretly.[97]

The Sacred Congregation acknowledged two schools of thought among canonists, the one maintaining, the other denying, the validity of an ordination performed by an abbot contrary to the restriction imposed by the Council of Trent. Fagnanus,[98] Tamburini (+ 1666),[99] Petra (1662-1747),[100] Riganti (1661-1735)[101]

[94] *Commentaria in Quinque Libros Decretalium* (5 vols., Coloniae Allobrogum, 1759), ad c. 4, X, *de consuetudine,* I, nn. 23-25.

[95] *Commentaria in Quinque Libros Decretalium,* ad c. 1, X, *de supplenda negligentia praelatorum,* I, n. 6.

[96] *Commentaria in Quinque Libros Decretalium,* ad c. 1, X, *de supplenda negligentia praelatorum,* I, n. 16, 33. Cf. *op. cit.,* ad c. 9, X, *de consecratione ecclesiae vel altaris,* III, n. 12.

[97] S. C. C., *Collen.,* 24 ian. 1795—*Thesaurus SCC,* LXIV, 4-7. For the reply only, cf. *Fontes,* n. 3892.

[98] *Loc. cit.*

[99] *De Jure Abbatum et Aliorum Praelatorum tam Regularium quam Secularium Episcopis Inferiorum* (3 vols., Coloniae Agrippinae, 1691), Tom. II, disput. II, quaest. VIII.

[100] *Commentaria ad Constitutiones Apostolicas* (5 vols., Venetiis, 1729), in const. IX (*Licet*) Pii II, n. 38-39.

[101] *Commentaria in Regulas, Constitutiones, et Ordinationes Cancellariae*

and Pope Benedict XIV (1740-1758)[102] held that the sacramental effect which was attached to the blessing received by the abbot enabled him to ordain validly even a non-subject.

The opposing school, which included Hallier (1595-1659),[103] Barbosa (1589-1649),[104] Pignatelli (+ after 1700),[105] and Leurenius (1646-1723)[106] held that the legislation of the Council of Trent not only had forbidden the abbot to use his power in regard to persons other than his Regular subjects, but also had actually taken away the faculty to ordain such candidates.

Hallier, to whose doctrine an appeal was made in the notes, explicitly distinguished between the abbatial blessing and the episcopal consecration. The latter imprinted on the bishop a sacramental character; if a bishop ordained a candidate who was not his subject, the ordination was valid because the power to ordain was intrinsically attached to the minister. On the other hand, an abbot did not obtain the power to ordain either from his priesthood, or from any sacramental character, since the blessing he received was not a sacrament. He obtained his power entirely in consequence of a privilege. The Council of Trent, by restricting his faculty to ordain, had limited the extent of his privilege. As far as secular candidates were concerned, he had no more power to ordain them than any priest. Hence any ordination attempted by an abbot on behalf of a secular subject was invalid, since there was nothing of a sacramental character which could supply the necessary power when the abbot exceeded his concession.[107]

On the basis of Hallier's explanations, the Sacred Congregation of the Council decided for the invalidity of the ordination.

Under Pope Pius IX (1846-1878) still another case was sub-

Apostolicae (4 vols., Coloniae Allobrogum, 1751), Regula XXIV, § III, n. 315.

[102] *De Synodo Diocesana*, lib. II, cap. 11, n. 11-13. Cf. ep. *"Ad audientiam,"* 15 febr. 1753, § 16—*Fontes*, n. 424.

[103] *De Sacris Electionibus*, Pars II, sect. V, cap. I, art. 2, n. 14-19.

[104] *De Officio et Potestate Episcopi* (2 vols., Lugduni, 1656), Pars II, Alleg. II, n. 11.

[105] *Consultationes Canonicae* (17 vols., Coloniae Allobrogum, 1700), Tom. I, Consult. 366, n. 2.

[106] *Forum Ecclesiasticum* (5 vols., Venetiis, 1729), lib. I, tit. xi, q. 562, n. 4.

[107] *Loc. cit.*

mitted to Rome for a solution. The reply served only to perpetuate the existing doubt. An abbot, at the request of the ordinand's bishop, had ordained one of the latter's subjects, as it had been the abbot's wont to do. The Sacred Congregation said nothing of reordination, but provided for the absolution of both the minister and the ordained, and simultaneously forbade the practice for the future.[108]

The Code has put an end to the doubts by carefully defining the extent of the regular abbot's power to ordain. A regular abbot *de regimine* can validly ordain only those candidates who are subject to him at least by simple profession.[109]

A religious can be subject to an abbot either by the act of religious profession or by a legitimate transfer from another monastery. For the relation of a religious to the abbot of the monastery to which the candidate belongs can be compared to the relations which exist between a father and a son. It is based, not on the existence of jurisdiction, but on the filiation which results from the act of profession.[110] Though the monk may come under the jurisdiction of a superior in a monastic congregation, he remains a true subject only of his own abbot. It is for this reason that superiors of the monastic congregation, and even the Abbot Primate, cannot in their own right ordain subjects of other abbots, even in the same order.[111]

The Code requires that the candidate be subject to the abbot by at least simple profession. Simple profession, temporary or perpetual,[112] is the minimum that satisfies the requirements; certainly, those who have made their solemn profession of vows may receive ordination from the abbot to whom they owe subjection through such a profession of vows.[113] Even though the action

---

[108] S. C. Ep. et Reg., *S. Hyppoliti*, 20 aug. 1852—Bizzarri, pp. 139-140.

[109] Canon 964, 1°.

[110] Gómez, "De Abbatum Potestate Tonsuram Minoresque Ordines Conferendi"—*CpR*, X (1929), 46-47.

[111] Cf. *supra*, pp. 71-72.

[112] Beste, *Introductio*, p. 511.

[113] Gasparri (*De Sacra Ordinatione*, n. 949), before the Code, favored the view that those who were in simple vows could not be ordained by the abbot since they were not strictly Regulars. Many (*De Sacra Ordinatione*,

would be illicit, it seems that an abbot would validly ordain a lay brother subject to him.[114] While an abbot, just as a bishop, is forbidden to ordain a candidate who is his subject if at the same time he belongs to another rite,[115] the ordination could be considered as valid.

On the other hand, those who are not subjects of the abbot by religious profession cannot be validly ordained by him. While most of the decisions already referred to clearly show that the Holy See wished to exclude both seculars and Regulars who were not subjects of the abbot from the ambit of his faculty to ordain,[116] it is not amiss to indicate several specific pre-Code rulings, which indicate that the abbot was not allowed to ordain such as are now commonly described as *familiares*.[117] While the abbot, as a major superior in a clerical exempt religious institute, can confer jurisdiction for the hearing of the confessions of such candidates,[118] and has also the right to administer to them the last sacraments,[119] they cannot be included among those for whom the abbot can exercise his power of ordination. Those who have not become his subjects by religious profession, such as oblates,[120] aspirants, postulants, novices,[121] as well as students[122] and guests, cannot now be validly ordained by him.

Nor can an abbot validly ordain others than his subjects by profession, even when they present dimissorials from their proper ordinary. For they do not thereby become the abbot's subjects by

---

n. 52, 3°) pointed out that since those who were in simple vows could receive ordination if the needed dimissorials had been issued by the abbot, there was no adequate reason why he himself could not ordain them. The Code clearly admits the latter view.

[114] S. C. C., *Congregationis Cisterciensis*, 28 nov. 1789—*Thesaurus SCC*, LVIII, 219-222.

[115] Canon 20; Regatillo, *Ius Sacramentarium*, II, n. 153.

[116] *Supra*, pp. 76 ff.

[117] Cf. canon 514, § 1.

[118] Canon 875, § 1.

[119] Canon 514, § 1.

[120] S. C. C., *Mutien.*, 14 maii 1689—Petra, *Commentaria ad Constitutiones Apostolicas*, in const. unica Urbani II, sect. 2, n. 21.

[121] He would also be forbidden to ordain a novice. Cf. canon 567, § 2.

[122] S. C. C., *Collen.*, 24 ian. 1795—*Fontes*, n. 3892. Cf. *supra*, p. 80.

profession.[123] The Abbot Primate, in virtue of his special faculty, can ordain subjects of other abbots, provided that the requisite dimissorial letters are furnished.[124]

Unless the abbot is a consecrated bishop, or unless he enjoys the power to ordain in virtue of another faculty, the Regular abbot *de regimine* can validly confer tonsure and minor orders only on candidates who are subject to him at least by simple profession.

While the restriction contained in the original grant of the II Council of Nicaea (787) as to the place of ordination is not reproduced in canon 964, 1°, abbots are indirectly restricted when at the ordination they make use of the pontifical insignia. This point is treated later, in connection with the discussion regarding the place of ordination.[125]

3. The Orders Conferred

A Regular abbot *de regimine,* just as the other extraordinary ministers described in the Code, can confer tonsure and the four minor orders.[126]

The II Council of Nicaea described the abuse whereby tonsured but not ordained monks were performing the office of the lector. Hence the superior was specifically granted only the faculty to confer the order of lector.[127] While tonsure was originally conferred at the same time and as a preliminary to the first ordination received by the candidate,[128] it was a separate rite when

[123] An abbot *nullius,* however, could perform an ordination of a non-subject if dimissorial letters are presented. He acts, however, not in his capacity as a religious superior, but as territorial prelate. Cf. Benko, *The Abbot Nullius,* pp. 74-75.

[124] *Supra,* p. 71.

[125] *Infra,* pp. 119 ff.

[126] Canon 964, 1°.

[127] Canon 14—Mansi, XIII, 433. It is interesting to note that the very practice which occasioned the origin of the abbatial power of ordination is now sanctioned, in that a tonsured cleric may function, with some limitations, even as a subdeacon. Cf. S. R. C., decr. 11 mar. 1906—*Decr. Auth.,* n. 4181; *Egitanien.,* 23 nov. 1602, ad 6—*Decr. Auth.,* n. 113; *Asculana,* 11 dec. 1885, ad 7—*Decr. Auth.,* n. 3647.

[128] Gasparri, *De Sacra Ordinatione,* n. 37; Morinus, *Commentarius de Sacris Ecclesiae Ordinationibus,* Pars II, p. 131.

conferred privately, as when young boys were dedicated to the clerical state.[129]

Pope Innocent III (1198-1216) ruled that tonsure could be conferred by an abbot on a layman.[130] The abbot's power to confer tonsure was not subsequently questioned, and is now specifically indicated in canon 964, 1°.

The glossators understood the power of the abbot to extend to the three minor orders of cantor, porter, and lector.[131] Since any priest could confer the office of cantor, even without the knowledge of the bishop,[132] there was no doubt about the power of an abbot to do so.[133] The office became obsolete in the Western Church. Even in the Greek Church, where both the lectorate and the subdiaconate are considered minor orders,[134] the cantor is ordained by means of the same ceremony as a lector, except that, at the conclusion of the rite, the cantor receives a book of the psalms, and the lector a book of the lessons.[135]

The order of porter was understood as included in the abbatial power of ordination, even though explicit mention of it was not made. For, it was argued, he who could confer a higher order (that of lector) could likewise confer an inferior order.[136]

Since the order of lector was the burden of the original grant, there was no difficulty as to the abbot's competence to confer it.

The extension of the superior's power to confer orders higher than that of the lectorate resulted from concessions made by law and by privilege. In the East, the conferring of the subdiaconate, which was there considered a minor order, was allowed to mon-

---

[129] Wernz, *Ius Decretalium* (6 vols., Romae, 1898-1905), II, n. 15. Cf. c. 5, D. XXVIII.

[130] C. 11, X, *de aetate et qualitate et ordine praeficiendorum*, I, 14; Potthast, n. 4072.

[131] *Glossa ordinaria* ad c. 1, D. LXIX, s.v. *tonsura vero.*

[132] C. 20, D. XXIII.

[133] *Glossa ordinaria* ad c. 20, D. XXIII, s.v. *sola.*

[134] II Council of Trullo (692), canon 6—Bruns, *Canones Apostolorum et Conciliorum Saeculorum* IV-VII (2 vols., Berolini, 1839), I, 39.

[135] Morinus, *op. cit.*, Pars II, p. 131; Pars III, Exer. XIV, c. 5. Cf. De Meester, *De Monachico Statu iuxta Disciplinam Byzantinam*, p. 19, 249-252.

[136] *Glossa ordinaria* ad c. 1, D. LXIX, s.v. *tonsura vero et lectoris; Glossa ordinaria* ad c. 3, *de privilegiis*, V, 7, in VI°, s.v. *tonsuram.*

astic superiors by the sixth canon attributed to Nicephorus I, Confessor (c. 758-829).[137]

In the West, it was admitted that the abbot could confer all four minor orders if he had a privilege to that effect. This, apparently, was not unusual, since Pope Alexander III (1159-1181) pointed out that minor orders and the subdiaconate could be conferred by those who were not bishops,[138] and, specifically, by abbots.[139] Pope Innocent IV (1243-1254) granted the abbots of the Benedictine monastery of St. Benedict at Mantua the privilege *in perpetuum* of conferring tonsure and the four minor orders.[140] Similarly Pope Martin IV (1281-1285) granted the abbots of St. Denis the privilege of conferring tonsure and the other minor orders on the subjects of that monastery.[141]

What is probably the extreme of privilege in this regard was granted by Pope Boniface IX (1389-1404) to the Augustinian monastery of St. Osyth. The Bull *"Sacrae Religionis"* (February 1, 1400) granted the abbot and his successors the privilege to confer not only tonsure and minor orders, but also sacred orders, inclusive of the priesthood. At the instance of Bishop Robert Braybrook of London, who enjoyed a *ius patronatus* in the abbey, the privilege was recalled in another Bull, *"Apostolicae Sedis"* (February 6, 1403).[142] It is said that, less than a century later, Pope Innocent VIII (1484-1492) granted the Cistercians the faculty under which their abbot general and the four major abbots were authorized to ordain monks to the diaconate inclusive. Gasparri (1852-1934) maintained that the Bull *"Exposcit"* (April

---

[137] *PG*, C, 855-856; Mansi, XIV, 123-126.

[138] C. 1, X, *de ordinatis ab episcopo qui renunciavit episcopatui*, I, 13; Jaffé, n. 14114.

[139] *Glossa ordinaria* ad c. 1, X, *de ordinatis ab episcopo qui renunciavit episcopatui*, I, 13, s.v. *a non episcopis*.

[140] Berger, *Les Registres d'Innocent IV* (4 vols., Paris, 1884-1897), 17 ian. 1251, n. 4972; Potthast, n. 14143 (18 dec. 1250).

[141] Martin, *Les Registeres de Martin IV* (Paris, 1901), n. 123; Potthast, n. 21866.

[142] The text of both documents is presented by Egerton Beck, "Two Bulls of Boniface IX for the Abbot of St. Osyth"—*The English Historical Review* (London, 1886-), XXVI (1911), 125-127. Cappello (*De Sacra Ordinatione*, n. 308-309) also reproduces them.

9, 1489), which contained that concession, was genuine, but that the grant did not extend to the conferring of the diaconate.[143] Both the grant of Pope Boniface IX and that of Pope Innocent VIII occasioned considerable discussion.[144] The fact nevertheless remains that the extension of the abbot's power to confer orders higher than that of the lectorate came by privilege.

The Council of Trent supposed that the abbot already had the faculty to confer tonsure and minor orders. It restricted the abbot, not as to the orders he might confer, but as to the persons he might ordain.[145]

By the law of the Code, a Regular abbot *de regimine* can confer only tonsure and the four minor orders. Even if he enjoyed a privilege, granted before the Code, which allowed him to confer orders higher than the last of the minor orders, that concession has now ceased, for the Code has recalled all contrary privileges. An abbot who is also a consecrated bishop can, of course, validly confer major orders.

The power of the abbot to ordain has been definitely stabilized by the Code. Unlike other religious superiors, he enjoys the power to ordain independently of episcopal consecration.[146]

In performing the ordinations, the abbot observes the formula in the Pontifical. It should be noted, however, that he does not pronounce the threat of censure as a bishop is wont to do before the ceremony begins.[147]

---

[143] *De Sacra Ordinatione*, n. 798.

[144] Cf. Cappello, *De Sacra Ordinatione*, n. 294-312; Wernz, *Ius Decretalium*, II, n. 27; Gerland, "Le Ministre Extraordinaire du Sacrement de l'Ordre"—*Revue Thomiste* (Paris, 1893-), XXXVI (1931), 874-885; Hugon, "Etudes Recentes sur le Sacrement de l'Ordre"—*Revue Thomiste*, XXIX (1924), 490-493.

[145] Conc. Trident., sess. XXIII, *de ref.*, c. 10. Cf. Cappello, *De Sacra Ordinatione*, n. 285.

[146] It may be interesting to compare canon 964, 1°, with the text of a similar faculty suggested by De Meester (*De Monachico Statu iuxta Disciplinam Byzantinam*, p. 19) for the Orientals: "Hegumenus quilibet, dummodo canonice sit institutus atque sacerdotio insignitus et chirothesiam ab Episcopo susceperit, potest in proprio monasterio monachos sibi subjectos lectores et psaltas necnon hypodiaconos ordinare."

[147] *Rituale Monasticum* (Collegeville, Minn.: Typis Abbatiae Sancti Joannis Baptistae, 1942), p. 468.

ARTICLE II. THE DIOCESAN BISHOP

If the religious candidate for orders does not receive ordination from his religious superior, he can be promoted only with the dimissorial letters of the superior. Unlike a bishop,[148] the religious superior is not free to direct these letters to any valid minister of orders, but must observe the procedure required by law. Some institutes enjoy a privilege which allows them to approach any bishop for the reception of orders. Since the Code has not recalled such special concessions, institutes which enjoyed the favor before the promulgation of the Code may continue to do so. In other cases the superior must direct the dimissorial letters to the bishop of the diocese in whose territory is located the religious house to whose *familia* the candidate belongs.[149]

A. *Historical Note*

The formulation of the prior right enjoyed by the diocesan bishop is a result developed after centuries of legislation. Already at the Council of Arles (455) the local bishop was recognized to have the exclusive right to ordain religious candidates, either personally or by employing the services of another.[150]

The early grants of exemption made to monasteries did not take away the episcopal prerogative to ordain candidates from such houses,[151] and specific mention of the bishop's right was made, as in the charters which conveyed the privilege of exemption to the abbey of St. Martin at Tours[152] and to the monastery at Bec in Normandy.[153]

The I General Council of the Lateran (1123) passed the first universal law which reserved among other functions, the con-

---

[148] Canon 961.

[149] Canon 965.

[150] Mansi, VII, 907-908.

[151] Thomassinus, *Vetus et Nova Ecclesiae Disciplina,* Pars I, lib. iii, c. xxx, n. 9; Hallier, *De Sacris Electionibus,* Pars II, Sect. V, Cap. III, art. 8, n. 5.

[152] This was granted by Pope Adeodatus II (672-676). Cf. *PL,* LXXXVII, 1143-1144; Jaffé, n. 2105.

[153] Cf. Mabillon, *Annales Ordinis S. Benedicti* (6 vols., Lucase, 1739-1745), Lib. LXVI, n. 31.

ferring of sacred orders to the local bishop.[154] Pope Boniface VIII (1294-1303) forbade a bishop to ordain a candidate who was not his subject unless he had the permission of the candidate's bishop; religious superiors, unless they had an indult, could not issue these general dimissorials.[155] While this legislation apparently restricted the choice of the ordaining prelate, even for religious, extant customs[156] and generous indults contravened the law.

Already in 1140, Peter the Venerable (1092-1156) mentioned that, in virtue of the largess of the Apostolic See, the monks of Cluny could obtain ordination from any Catholic bishop.[157] Pope Alexander III (1159-1181), in his grant of privileges to the abbey at Monte Cassino, listed the favor of allowing monks of that abbey to receive their ordination from any bishop they might select.[158] Because of their centralized organization and frequent change of residence, the Friars Minor obtained a similar privilege from Pope Clement IV (1265-1268),[159] which was confirmed by other pontiffs to Pope Sixtus IV (1471-1484).[160] The Order of Friars Preachers enjoyed a similar grant.[161] Through the acknowledged agency of the reciprocal participation in privileges, these grants were shared by the other orders. The very granting of these favors, however, recognized the right of the local bishop in relation to which they were constituted as an exception.

At the V General Council of the Lateran (1512-1517), Pope Leo X (1513-1521) sought to restore order and uniformity in the choice of ordaining prelates. The Constitution *"Dum intra"*

---

[154] Canon 17—Mansi, XXI, 285; c. 10, C. XVI, q. 1.

[155] C. 3, *de temporibus ordinationum et qualitate ordinandorum,* I, 9, in VI°.

[156] *Glossa ordinaria* ad c. 3, *de temporibus ordinationum et qualitate ordinandorum,* I, 9, in VI° s.v. *indultum.*

[157] Mabillon, *Annales Ordinis. S. Benedicti,* Lib. LXXVII, n. 84.

[158] Const. *"Licet omnium,"* 7 nov. 1159—*Bull. Rom. Taur.,* II, 663; Jaffé, n. 10594.

[159] Const. *"Virtute conspicuos,"* 21 iul. 1265—*Bull. Rom. Taur.,* III, 737; Potthast, n. 19280.

[160] Const. *"Regimini universalis,"* 31 aug. 1474—*Bull. Rom. Taur.,* V, 224-225.

[161] Gregory XI, const. *"Virtute conspicuos,"* 6 mart. 1374—*Bull. Rom. Taur.,* IV, 568.

required that the religious candidate for ordination receive his orders from the diocesan bishop or his vicar, unless the bishop unreasonably refused to perform the ordination or was absent from the diocese.[162]

The Council of Trent (1545-1563) gave considerable attention to the determination of the proper bishop for ordination. It first repeated the former law, which required that each candidate was to be ordained by his own bishop,[163] who, except in the case of illness, was personally to confer the orders.[164] Should the candidate enjoy the faculty of being ordained *a quocumque,* this was of no value without a legitimate reason stated in writing by the ordinand's bishop.[165] All ordinations were to take place in the bishop's own diocese, or, if in another diocese, with the permission of the local ordinary, and only for his subjects.[166] Titular bishops could ordain non-subjects who had the permission of their ordinary.[167]

A controversy arose on the point whether the privileges which allowed Regulars to seek ordination from any bishop whatsoever were recalled. For, though their privileges were contrary to the legislation of the Council regarding the authority for promotion by anyone, that provision did not recall or contradict specifically any contrary privilege.[168] Since Pope Pius IV (1559-1565) recalled the privileges which stood in opposition to, but not also those which reflected a divergence from, the legislation of the Council,[169] Regulars maintained that their privileges to obtain ordination from any bishop whatsoever remained intact. Pope Pius V (1566-1572) declared that the provisions of the Council of Trent regarding the authority for promotion by anyone were not applicable to Regulars, and that therefore they could continue to use these privileges as before.[170]

---

[162] 19 dec. 1516, § 11—*Bull. Rom. Taur.*, V, 687; *Fontes,* n. 72.

[163] Conc. Trident., sess. XXIII, *de ref.* c. 8.

[164] Conc. Trident., sess. XXIII, *de ref.*, c. 3.

[165] Conc. Trident., sess. VII, *de ref.*, c. 11.

[166] Conc. Trident., sess. VI, *de ref.*, c. 5.

[167] Conc. Trident., sess. XIV, *de ref.*, c. 2.

[168] Conc. Trident., sess. VII, *de ref.*, c. 11

[169] Const. *"In principis Apostolorum Sede,"* 18 febr. 1564—*Bull. Rom. Taur.*, VII, 277-279.

[170] Const. *"Etsi mendicantium,"* 16 maii 1567, § 2—*Bull. Rom. Taur.*, VII, 584.

His successor, Pope Gregory XIII (1572-1585), soon after his election, revoked the privileges of Regulars on seeking orders from any bishop whatsoever, and required them to observe the Tridentine norm.[171] In the same year (1573), the Sacred Congregation of the Council ruled that some Carthusian monks, who had asked whether they might receive ordination from the bishop of another diocese, needed to have the express permission of the bishop of the diocese in which they were before they could approach another bishop.[172] The rule, therefore, was that Regulars were bound to receive orders from the bishop in whose diocese was located the monastery in which they resided.[173]

The first modification of the Tridentine law was to allow Regulars to approach any other bishop in the absence of the local bishop.[174] Shortly afterwards, Pope Sixtus V (1585-1590) reviewed the entire discipline of the ordination of Regulars, and through the Sacred Congregation of the Council ruled that Regulars should issue dimissorial letters for their candidates to the local bishop, unless he was absent or would not hold an ordination.[175]

This legislation received its definitive form under Pope Clement VIII (1592-1605). Through a decree of the Sacred Congregation of the Council, the "Clementine decree" as it was commonly called, the Pontiff ruled that thenceforth religious superiors were to direct dimissorial letters for the ordination of their subjects to the diocesan bishop, that is, the bishop of the territory in which was situated the monastery in whose *familia* the Regular had been placed by his superiors. If the bishop was absent or was not to hold ordinations, dimissorial letters could be addressed to any other bishop.[176] If the Regulars resided in a monastery *nullius*

---

[171] Const. "*In tanta rerum,*" 1 mart. 1573—*Bull. Rom. Taur.*, VIII, 39-41.

[172] S. C. C., *Ordinis Carthusian.*, anno 1573—quoted by Benedict XIV, const. "*Impositi Nobis,*" 27 febr. 1747, § 3—*Fontes*, n. 376.

[173] S. C. C., *Brugnaten.*, 17 maii 1589—Pallottini, s.v. *Sacramentum Ordinis*, III, n. 47.

[174] S. C. C., *Hispanarum*, mense sept. 1589—*Fontes*, n. 2216.

[175] As stated by Pope Benedict XIV, const. "*Impositi Nobis,*" 27 febr. 1747, § 4—*Fontes*, n. 376. Cf. S. C. C., *Catanien.*, 26 ian. 1595—*Fontes*, n. 2280.

[176] S. C. C., decr. 15 mart. 1596—*Fontes*, n. 2294.

dioecesis, they were to consider the bishop of the diocese nearest their monastery as the proper bishop for their ordinations, and they were to observe all details in regard to him as if he were their diocesan bishop.[177]

Since the legislation of Pope Clement VIII was not being observed in Spain,[178] Pope Innocent XIII (1721-1724) urged that it be observed there too, and further required that the diocesan bishop announce by edict his intention to hold an ordination.[179] Pope Benedict XIII reaffirmed this legislation for Spain.[180] He also reiterated the Clementine legislation and urged its observance by all bishops and Regulars.[181] The Sacred Congregation of the Council, too, insisted on the observance of the Clementine norm.[182]

Pope Benedict XIV (1740-1758), in his Constitution *"Impositi Nobis,"* treated the determination of the proper bishop for the ordination of Regulars at great length. After treating of the history of the problem from the time of the Council of Trent, he repeated the norm established under Pope Clement VIII and insisted upon its observance.[183] The provisions of this constitution also modified the procedure to be observed when some other bishop than the diocesan episcopal ordinary was approached. That consideration will be referred to at a later point.[184]

Until the time of the Code, the legislation of the *"Impositi Nobis"* remained as the common law for the ordination of Regulars. That, together with the Clementine decree, forms what is substantially reproduced in canons 965-967.

B. *Determination of the Proper Bishop*

The bishop to whom the religious superior is to direct the dimissorial letters is the bishop of the diocese in which is located the

---

[177] S. C. C., *Nullius,* 22 sept. 1600—*Fontes,* n. 2334.
[178] Benedictus XIV, *Institutiones Ecclesiasticae,* XXIII.
[179] Const. *"Apostolici ministerii,"* 23 maii 1723, § 17—*Fontes,* n. 280.
[180] Const. *"In supremo,"* 23 sept. 1724, § 14—*Fontes,* n. 283.
[181] Const. *"Pastoralis officii,"* 27 mart. 1726, § 3-5—*Fontes,* n. 292.
[182] S. C. C., *Brixien.,* 28 nov., 12 dec. 1733, ad III-V—*Fontes,* n. 3411.
[183] 27 febr. 1747—*Fontes,* n. 376.
[184] *Infra,* p. 117.

religious house to whose *familia* the ordinand belongs.[185] While the present law resembles greatly the Clementine decree, it is not without some pertinent modification. It should be noted that the canon describes the diocesan bishop, not as having the right to ordain the religious, but rather as having the right to receive dimissorial letters for their ordination. While this can be considered primarily a means used for the purpose of giving expression to the exclusive control enjoyed by the religious superior in determining whether his subjects are suitable candidates for ordination, it also provides a legal explanation why the religious superior who has the necessary power of orders can himself promote his subjects to orders.[186]

As in the pre-Code law, so in canon 965, the bishop who has the right to receive the dimissorial letters for the ordination of an exempt religious candidate is not determined directly by any personal relations, past or present, between the bishop and the candidate, but indirectly, through the location of the religious house to which the candidate belongs. It is the bishop of that diocese in which is located the religious house of which the ordinand is a member that has the right to receive the dimissorial letters.

It is necessary that the religious house be a true canonical religious house, that is, such as has been established according to the prescribed canonical formalities. In order to be considered a canonically established religious house, it must be constituted by a competent superior acting with the written permission of the local ordinary and of the Holy See.[187] This determines it as a collegiate moral personality,[188] a feature absent in a simple residence which, even though it be intended for use exclusively by religious, does not enjoy the juridic status of a religious house. Such dwellings have no need for a formal and canonical estab-

---

[185] Canon 965: Episcopus ad quem Superior religiosus litteras dimissorias mittere debet, est Episcopus dioecesis, in qua sita est domus religiosa, ad cuius familiam pertinet ordinandus.

[186] *Supra,* pp. 66-67.

[187] Canon 497, § 1.

[188] Coronata, *Institutiones,* I, n. 504; Beste, *Introductio,* p. 313.

lishment.[189] The religious living at such a residence do not form a community, nor does the bishop in whose diocese such a house is located acquire the right to receive dimissorial letters for the ordination of candidates dwelling there.

The religious, to be ordained by the bishop proper to the religious house, must belong to its *familia*. When canon 965 is compared with the text of the Clementine decree,[190] the use of practically the same words, though in a different manner, allows one to overlook the present clarification of the law. According to the Clementine decree, the relationship of the candidate to the monastery which determined the ordaining bishop was described as that in the family of which the Regular was placed, by those who were competent to do so. The present canon omits all reference to the manner in which the candidate's membership in the house arises, and considers only the fact that he belongs to the *familia* of the religious house. This change is made more difficult to detect, for in the former law *pertinet* indicated the subjection of the religious to his superior, whereas now it describes his membership in the religious house.

Though the law prescribes that a religious normally live in a religious house of his institute,[191] it is left to the nature of the organization and to its particular laws to determine the manner in which membership in a definite house arises. In decentralized religious institutes the act of profession and usually a vow of stability incorporate the religious into a determinate house,[192] from which he can be transferred only with the permission of the Holy See.[193] Wherever the religious may be, he remains attached to the house of his profession. It is possible that the candidate has never even seen the monastery to which he belongs. Never-

---

[189] Vermeersch, *Epitome*, I, n. 607; Beste, *Introductio*, p. 325.

[190] Congregatio Concilii censuit superiores regulares posse . . . litteras dimissorias concedere, ad episcopum tamen dioecesanum, nempe illius monasterii in cuius familia ab iis ad quos pertinet, regularis positus fuerit. . . . S. C. C., decr. 15 mart. 1596—*Fontes*, n. 2294.

[191] Canon 606, § 2.

[192] André-Wagner, *Dictionnaire de Droit Canonique* (13. ed., 4 vols., Paris, 1901), s.v. "Ordre," § V, n. 2.

[193] Canon 632.

theless, the proper bishop for the receipt of the dimissorial letters in this type of institute is the bishop of the diocese in which is located the monastery for which the religious has made profession.

In centralized religious institutes the members, in virtue of their profession, belong to the entire institute or to one of its provinces. With such religious their membership in a particular house is usually effected through an act of assignment by the superior.[194] The scope and extent of the superior's power, as well as the formalities which necessarily must accompany such an assignment, are usually prescribed by the constitutions. Generally a formal letter or precept is specified.

The assignment, however, should effect an incorporation of the religious into the *familia* of the particular house, so that he can be said to belong to the house, to be *de familia.*[195] Simple residence, even at a formally established house, does not necessarily give rise to actual membership in the community of the religious who are assigned to that house. Since there is no true membership, such residence would not determine the proper bishop who is to receive the dimissorial letters for the ordination of the religious involved. Thus, if the religious resides at some house of study, but does not belong to it, the dimissorial letters for his ordination are not to be directed to the bishop of that diocese on the simple basis of his residence in it.[196]

This doctrine was upheld in 1922 by the Sacred Congregation of Religious in the solution of a question submitted on behalf of the Benedictine abbots. Since monks are sometimes sent to another abbey or house of studies to complete their education for ordination, there arose a doubt as to which bishop could lawfully receive dimissorial letters for their ordination. By their profession they belonged to one abbey, while actually they were resident in another. If simple residence was sufficient as a factor for determining the bishop to whom the dimissorials were to be sent, there would have been no need for the Sacred Congregation to suggest that the Holy Father be petitioned to grant the faculty

194 André-Wagner, *loc. cit.*

195 Cf. canons 965; 995, § 1.

196 Villien, "L' Ordination"—*Le Canoniste Contemporain,* XLV (1922), 104.

that dimissorial letters might be addressed to the bishop of the place where the house of study was located.[197]

Simple residence, even in good faith, may not be invoked as the criterion for determining the proper bishop to receive the dimissorial letters for the ordination of a religious candidate. Actual membership is necessary.

Sometimes the religious remains formally affiliated with the principal or some other house of the institute while he is on leave for the purpose of study. In such cases the proper bishop to receive the dimissorial letters is the bishop of the diocese in which this house of affiliation is located.

But it can occur that the religious, though professed for the institute, is not assigned as a member of any house. This can be the case in those institutes which have not as yet developed a house of studies, so that the religious are sent to the diocesan seminary or to another religious institute to prepare for the priesthood.[198]

The pre-Code discipline provided that the dimissorial letters for such a candidate who lacked assignment to a house of the institute be directed to the bishop of the diocese in the seminary of which the candidate was studying, provided that the candidate had spent a full year there. Pope Leo XIII (1878-1903) promulgated this arrangement to be observed as law in such circumstances.[199]

Since the same situation can arise under the present law, the applicability of the pre-Code legislation should be considered. Some canonists maintain that the former norm is applicable, since the decree of the Sacred Congregation was simply an interpretation of the Clementine law. Since canon 965 reproduces what was

---

[197] S. C. de Religiosis, declar. 12 dec. 1922, ad II, III—*Annales OSB*, XXVIII-XXXIV (1920-1926), 100-101. In this declaration is contained the text of the faculty granted by Pope Benedict XV on November 25, 1922. By it the major superior in a Benedictine house may address the dimissorial letters for the ordination of monks subject to them to the bishop of the place in which the candidate is staying for the purpose of studies.

[198] Cf. canon 587, § 4.

[199] S. C. Ep. et Reg., decr. 7 iun. 1899—*ASS*, XXXVII (1904-1905), 240-241.

essentially the Clementine decree, the 1899 ruling remains applicable in consequence of the legal principle enunciated in canon 6, 2°.[200]

While this opinion merits attention because of the extrinsic authority of those who advance it, their arguments are contrary to the facts. The decree of the Sacred Congregation was not a reply to a question which involved the Clementine decree; it was a new norm enacted to supplement the existing legislation. The decree was a law approved as such by the Holy Father.[201] It should not be treated, therefore, as a clarification of canon 965, but rather as a law which was not reenacted in the Code, and, therefore, no longer applicable.[202] The abrogation of this law of 1899 could also be argued from the fact that the basis it proposed as the criterion for determining the proper bishop, viz., residence protracted over a year, is contrary to the present law which requires membership in the community.[203]

If it were assumed that the law was still applicable, that fact would present a difficulty in the preparation of the dimissorial letters. For the superior must attest to the fact that the candidate is *de familia* of a religious house subject to him, a statement manifestly impossible if the ordinand does not belong to any religious house of the institute.

Had simple residence of this type been sufficient, the need for insisting that the ordinand belong to a definite house would be pointless; it seems clear that the legislator did not intend to allow such freedom in the determination of the ordaining prelate.

Unless the candidate for orders is attached to some religious house of his institute, it seems that no provision is made in the Code for determining the proper bishop to receive the dimissorial

---

[200] (Anonymous) "De Ordinatione Religiosorum, Quod ad Episcopum Proprium"—*Periodica,* XIV (1925) (52)-(53). Schaaf refers to this article, but without further comment. Cf. "Episcopus Proprius Ordinationis Religiosorum"—*The Ecclesiastical Review* (Philadelphia, 1889-1943; *The American Ecclesiastical Review,* Washington, 1944-), XC (1934), 497-498 (hereafter cited *ER, AER*).

[201] Many, *De Sacra Ordinatione,* n. 181.

[202] Canon 6, 6°.

[203] Cf. canon 6, 1°.

letters for his ordination. Institutes in which this problem does arise may approach the Holy See for an indult suited to their particular situation.

It should be noted that it is the house to which the candidate is attached, not that to which the superior belongs, which determines the proper bishop. Even though the superior and the candidate are in different dioceses, it is the bishop of the diocese in which is located the religious house to which the candidate belongs that has the right to receive the dimissorial letters.

The dimissorial letters are to be addressed by the religious superior to the bishop of the diocese. While this is ordinarily the residential bishop,[204] the expression is actually broader in meaning and includes certain persons whose authority is equivalent to or a substitute for that of the residential bishop. The concepts of bishop of the diocese and of local ordinary are not, however, identical; while all residential bishops are indeed local ordinaries, not all local ordinaries are diocesan bishops.[205] Through the interpretation furnished by jurisprudence, the expression "bishop of the diocese" has acquired a technical connotation in regard to the ordination of exempt religious. Hence the full implication of the phrase cannot be learned exclusively from the text of the Code.

Primarily, the bishop of the diocese is its residential bishop, who has the right to receive dimissorial letters for the ordination of the exempt religious who belong to religious houses located in his diocese. It is not necessary, however, that he shall personally perform the ordinations. He can, under certain circumstances, entrust this to another without losing his right to receive the letters. As will be shown later, the bishop is considered as ordaining even though the rites are performed by another.[206] The minister thus empowered to act ordains not in his own name but in virtue of the authority received from the diocesan bishop. Ordinarily, the coadjutor and auxiliary bishops assist the residential bishop in this respect.[207] However, the bishop may invite others who are not thus attached to him or to his diocese. In any case, the right

---

[204] Canon 334, § 1.

[205] Canon 198.

[206] *Infra,* p. 114.

[207] Canons 351, § 4; 352.

to receive the dimissorial letters accrues only to the residential bishop, unless, for one of the reasons stated in canon 966, § 1, this right is forfeited.

In certain circumstances the Holy See institutes in a diocese an authority who is the equivalent of the residential bishop. To those who occupy such a position all the rights of the diocesan bishop accrue. Such is an apostolic administrator who is appointed to rule a diocese *sede plena,* unless the letters of appointment provide otherwise.[208] Likewise a coadjutor bishop *datus personae,* if the residential bishop is entirely incapacited, has the rights of the bishop of the diocese, unless the letters of appointment state differently.[209]

In territories not organized as dioceses, vicars and prefects apostolic,[210] and abbots and prelates *nullius,*[211] enjoy the same rights as a bishop in his diocese. Even though they are not bishops, they have the power to confer tonsure and minor orders on such as present legitimate dimissorial letters.[212] For exempt religious who belong to houses located in the territory subject to these prelates, the major religious superior must direct the dimissorial letters for the ordination of their candidates to these prelates.

Whenever references are made to the diocesan bishop, they are applicable to those who are constituted as apostolic administrators and as coadjutors to the person of the residential bishop, as just explained, and also to the prelate who governs a territory which is not a diocese.

The right to receive the dimissorial letters for the ordination of the exempt religious of the diocese is acquired by the diocesan bishop, or by the prelate who enjoys an equivalent authority, from the time he takes canonical possession of the office,[213] and the possession of that right continues for the duration of the bishop's

---

[208] Canons 314, 315, § 1-2, with 435, § 2. If the see is vacant, the provisions of canon 966, § 1, determine the rights of the administrator.

[209] Canon 351, § 1-2.

[210] Canon 294, § 1.

[211] Canon 215, § 2.

[212] Canon 957. Cf. *supra,* pp. 65-66.

[213] Canons 334, § 2-3; 293, § 2; 322, § 1; 313, § 1; 353.

or prelate's incumbency in his office. When the office becomes vacant, the provisions of canon 966, § 1, become applicable.

C. *Cautions Against Fraud*

The prerogative of the diocesan bishop to receive the dimissorial letters for the ordination of the exempt religious in his diocese could easily become reduced to an empty claim, either through the transfer of the candidates to religious houses in other dioceses, or through a postponement in the granting of the dimissorial letters to a time when the bishop is expected to be absent, or when it can be assumed that he will not hold ordinations. For, by being incorporated into another religious house in a different diocese, the candidate is thereby assigned another bishop relative to the matter of ordination, and when dimissorial letters are to be granted while the bishop is absent or unwilling to hold an ordination, they may be sent to another bishop.[214]

Since both the transfer of religious from one house to another and the granting of dimissorial letters are reserved to the religious superior, it is possible for him to exercise these rights, either for a just and reasonable reason, or for the unworthy purpose of evading the claims of a particular bishop. The law therefore cautions religious superiors against this unbecoming motive, and forbids them to undertake an unauthorized transfer or to resort to an undue procrastination. Such an action would connote the perpetration of fraud on the diocesan bishop.[215] The violation of this law is punished with the vindictive penalty of a month's suspension from the celebrating of Holy Mass. This penalty is incurred automatically upon the expediting of dimissorial letters which connote the presence of such fraud.[216]

The text of the Clementine decree could be given an interpretation which allowed the superior, even in bad faith, to address dimissorial letters to the bishop in whose diocese was located the monastery to which the candidate had been assigned. Pope Benedict XIV condemned such a practice, and threatened with

[214] Canon 966, § 1.

[215] Canon 967.

[216] Canon 2410. Cf. *infra*, p. 127.

penalties those superiors who made themselves guilty of such an abuse. For the intent of the Clementine law was that Regulars be ordained by the bishop in whose territory they had their domicile.[217]

Canonists, too, recognized the possibility of a fraudulent transfer in line with a purely literal interpretation of the Clementine decree. Against such sophistry they urged the concept of a domicile acquired by assignment as the criterion which determined the proper bishop for the reception of the dimissorial letters. Transitory residence was insufficient, they held, for the acquiring of the requisite domicile. Consequently a temporary stay at a house did not authorize that bishop to admit the candidate to orders.[218] Furthermore, they averred, the effected transfer met the demands of the law when the assignment was made in good faith, that is, with the intention of incorporating the religious into the house.[219] Only in such cases was the candidate *de familia* of the monastery, so that he could be licitly promoted to orders by the bishop of the diocese in which that house was situated.[220]

The length of time during which the religious was actually resident in the religious house was not the criterion of whether he was truly a member. Thus, in one case in which the candidate had resided in the religious house for only four days, it became allowable for him to be promoted to orders by the bishop of the diocese in which that religious house was located.[221] Apparently the attitude of pre-Code canonists was that a religious, by assignment to a definite house, acquired a domicile, and that on the strength of this permanent residence was assigned a proper bishop for ordination.

Though the present law prescinds from a consideration of domicile as a basis for determining the proper bishop, a fraudulent transfer is nevertheless possible. However, the assignment of a proper bishop for ordination is intimately associated with the

---

[217] Const. "*Impositi Nobis,*" 27 febr. 1747, § 15—*Fontes,* n. 376.

[218] Van Espen, *Jus Ecclesiasticum Universum,* Lib. II, tit. 9, n. 39.

[219] Passerinus, *De Hominum Statibus et Officiis* (3 vols., Lucae, 1732), Q. CLXXXIX, art. x, n. 814.

[220] Honorante, *Praxis Secretariae Tribunalis Cardinalis Urbis Vicarii* (2. ed., Romae, 1762), C. XII, not. 2.

[221] S. C. C., *Neapolitana,* 8 aug. 1691—Honorante, *loc. cit.*

candidate's membership in the *familia* of a particular house. If anything, the present law expresses more clearly and demands more precisely what was to be understood in the pre-Code discipline. Obviously, a transfer from one house to another is possible in only those institutes in which a religious belongs to a definite house through an act of assignment on the part of the superior, and not in consequence of the act of the religious profession itself.

All that is required for membership in a given house in such institutes is that the religious be assigned to it by the superior with the intention that the subject belong to it as a regular member.[222]

Superiors have the right, within the limits of their office, to assign their subjects to other houses for just and reasonable causes, such as the prosecution of study or the recuperation of health. They thus discharge the duties of their office by providing for the welfare of the institute and of the individual members, even though indirectly a particular bishop may be deprived of his prerogative in regard to a particular member. On the contrary, when the superior effects the change to defraud the bishop of his right, he acts unjustly and is liable to the penalties enacted in the law.[223]

Just as the transfer of a religious candidate to another house deprives a bishop of the possibility of ordaining that particular candidate, so too the bishop is eluded through a postponement of the granting of the dimissorial letters to a time when he will be absent from the diocese or when he will not be holding ordinations. Under such circumstances the law considers his right to expect dimissorial letters as forfeited.[224]

Under the Clementine decree, if a superior had fraudulently withheld the preparation of the dimissorial letters, he could not

[222] Pejška, *Ius Canonicum Religiosorum,* pp. 303-304; Blat, *Commentarium Textus Codicis Iuris Canonici,* III, i, n. 313. An interesting comparison, which reflects the clarification of the present law, may be noted between Wernz (*Ius Decretalium,* II, i. n. 28) and Wernz-Vidal (*Ius Canonicum,* IV, i, n. 197). While both texts read ". . . in quo . . . promovendus habitat," the latter adds the significant words: "ut verum membrum illius communitatis."

[223] Blat, *ibid.,* n. 315.

[224] Canon 966, § 1.

subsequently direct them to another bishop.[225] By the law of the Code, a religious superior who has delayed the granting of the dimissorial letters in a manner that connotes the defrauding of the right of the diocesan bishop incurs the penalty enacted in canon 2410 when he directs the letters to another bishop.

Once again, the superior can refuse to prepare dimissorial letters when a sufficient and a reasonable cause is present, such as the failure of the candidate to pass the required examinations in his theological studies.[226] The superior offends only if the delay is motivated by the intention of depriving the diocesan bishop of his right. The penalty is not incurred, however, until the dimissorial letters have been sent to another bishop upon the superior's purposive delay with a view to depriving the diocesan bishop of his established right.[227]

The right of the diocesan bishop under the Code remains substantially the same as before its promulgation. He has the right to receive the dimissorial letters for the ordination of those exempt religious who belong to religious houses which are located in his diocese. Should the religious superior fail to recognize this right, or through fraudulent means cancel out its potential operation to which the bishop has a rightful claim, the superior then incurs the penalty which the law has enacted in canon 2410.

ARTICLE III. OTHER MINISTERS

While the right to receive dimissorial letters for the ordination of the exempt religious of his diocese is a prerogative of the diocesan bishop, there can and there do arise conditions which would cause undue hardship if the law allowed no exceptions. Unlike a bishop, who may for any just reason send his subjects to any other bishop for the reception of orders,[228] a religious superior does not have the same liberty for the simple reason that normally he must select the diocesan bishop as the minister of the orders to be conferred. But the present law lists five occasions on which it

[225] S. C. C., decr. 15 mart. 1596—*Fontes*, n. 2294.

[226] Prümmer, *Manuale Iuris Canonici*, Q. 246.

[227] Canon 2410. Cf. Blat, *loc. cit.*

[228] Canon 955; Cappello, *De Sacra Ordinatione*, n. 339.

becomes permissible for the religious superior to exercise considerable freedom without infringing on the basic right of the diocesan bishop.

A. *Excusing Causes*

The five reasons which allow the religious superior to direct the dimissorial letters to some bishop other than the diocesan episcopal ordinary, as listed in canon 966, § 1,[229] are the only causes that are admitted, as is evident from the word *tantum*. The list given there is an exhaustive listing; yet any one of the five enumerated causes constitute a sufficient reason.[230] With the exception of the first of these reasons, which is an act of permission granted by the bishop, the others do not require the bishop to waive his right; the very presence of the condition, if it be legitimately proved, is in itself a sufficient reason for the religious superior to direct the dimissorial letters to another bishop.

Since the obligation concerns the act of granting the dimissorial letters, the reason must be in existence at the time the dimissorial letters are issued. For the superior enjoys the right to direct them to another bishop only when one of the five reasons is present. Consequently, this suffices that the letters be legitimately prepared, even though it is foreseen that the condition will have ceased before the ordination takes place.

When one of the five occasions allows the superior to approach some other bishop than the diocesan episcopal ordinary, no restriction is imposed by the law as to which bishop is to be selected or even preferred, except that the minister is to be of the same rite as the ordinand.[231] It seems also that the selected minister could be an extraordinary minister if it is a matter of promotion to minor orders. For otherwise the concessions made to cardinals,[232]

[229] Tunc tantum Superior religiosus ad alium Episcopum litteras dimissorias mittere potest, cum Episcopus dioecesanus licentiam dederit, aut sit diversi ritus, aut sit absens, aut non sit ordinationem habiturus proximo legitimo tempore ad normam can. 1006, § 2, vel denique cum dioecesis vacet nec eam regat qui charactere episcopali polleat.

[230] Augustine, *Commentary*, IV, 440.

[231] Vermeersch-Creusen, *Epitome*, II, n. 241.

[232] Pejška, *Ius Canonicum Religiosorum*, p. 303.

to vicars and prefects apostolic, to abbots and prelates *nullius*, and to the Abbot Primate of the Benedictines, would be only nominal if the minister of necessity had to be a consecrated bishop.

The diocesan bishop who normally receives the dimissorial letters does not have the right to determine the minister to whom the superior may direct the candidates, except in the case wherein he grants his permission that another bishop be approached, or, indirectly, if the ordinations will take place within his diocese and he concedes the right to pontificate to no other bishop than the one designated by him. In the former case, since the bishop retains the right to concede or to refuse the request of the superior to approach another bishop, there seems no reasonable objection if he restricts his permission within determined limits.[233] In the latter case, by refusing to allow another bishop to ordain within his diocese, he can effectively, though indirectly, restrict the superior in the choice of the minister.[234]

1. Permission of the Diocesan Bishop

The exclusive right of the diocesan bishop to receive the dimissorial letters for the ordination of exempt religious assigned to houses in his diocese is a prerogative which he can waive. Before the Code this possibility was not definitely formulated as is done in the present law. Yet it was admitted as an application of the juridical rule that allowed the possessor of a right to forego its use.[235] At least one reply of the Sacred Congregations required the permission of the diocesan bishop if Regular superiors wished their subjects to be ordained by another bishop.[236] However, neither the Clementine decree nor the Constitution *Impositi Nobis* made reference to the use of the bishop's permission as a sufficient rea-

---

[233] Coronata, *De Sacramentis,* II, n. 45.

[234] Canons 337, § 1; 1008.

[235] Reg. 72, R. J., in VI°. Thus Many (*De Sacra Ordinatione*, n. 159) required that the bishop's permission be obtained by a religious superior who wished to ordain his own subjects.

[236] S. C. C., anno 1573—quoted by Benedict XIV, const. "*Impositi Nobis,*" 27 febr. 1747, § 3—*Fontes,* n. 376. Coronata (*De Sacramentis,* II, n. 45) and Augustine (*Commentary,* IV, 440) claim that no mention of this cause was made in previous documents.

son to approach another bishop. This can hardly be cited as evidence that this cause is an innovation in the Code, since these two documents make specific mention only of the bishop's absence or failure to hold an ordination.

This permission is a waiver of the diocesan bishop's right to receive the dimissorial letters. The Code does not require any reason for the bishop to make this concession, and it appears that the benevolence of the bishop towards the religious institute or towards religious in general suffices.[237] The permission is an act of grace which is not due to the religious, but for which they are at liberty to ask.

Since this permission is a favor which the bishop can withhold or grant, there seems to be no reason why he cannot limit it.[238] Thus he could place licit conditions, for example, in reference to the time and place of the ordination, to the orders which may be conferred, and to the ministers and candidates for ordination. There likewise seems to be no reason for any objections to his granting this permission for more than one occasion, if he so sees fit.

2. Difference in Rite

While the interritual discipline of the Church is generous in allowing members of one rite to receive Holy Communion and go to confession in a rite other than their own, this same liberty is not allowed in the reception of Holy Orders.[239] However, the provision that orders are to be received in the candidate's rite has not always existed in the general law of the Church. Pope Celestine III (1191-1198) objected, not to the ordination of members of the Greek rite by members of the Latin rite, and vice versa, but to the fact that the customs of the rites were being intermingled. He specifically objected to the failure to observe the proper times for ordinations.[240] Pope Innocent III (1198-1216) insisted that a Latin

---

[237] Coronata, *De Sacramentis*, II, n. 45.

[238] Coronata, *loc. cit.*

[239] Canon 955, § 2. Cf. canon 866; 905.

[240] *Ad Hydruntinum Archiepiscopum*—Jaffé, n. 17629. The portion of this letter which appears in the Decretals, as well as the title to that fragment, imply a prohibition of all interritual ordinations. Cf. c. 9, X, *de temporibus ordinationum et qualitate ordinandorum*, I, 11.

bishop should ordain his Greek rite subjects personally, and not send them to be ordained by Greek bishops.[241] Pope Clement VIII (1592-1605) appears to have given Latin bishops the option of ordaining Greek rite candidates personally, or of sending them with dimissorial letters to the Greek rite bishop stationed at Rome for this purpose.[242]

In constituting a Greek Melchite monastery, Pope Clement XII (1730-1740) directed that the candidates be promoted to orders by the Greek bishop.[243] Similarly, Pope Benedict XIV (1740-1758) insisted that among the Italo-Greeks, each candidate be promoted in his own rite, unless by special permission of the Holy See he might be promoted in another.[244] Canonists accepted the difference of rite as a sufficient reason for the religious superior to direct the dimissorial letters to a bishop other than the diocesan bishop, even though no specific provision of the law required this.[245]

Difference in rite is now an approved canonical reason for approaching some other than the diocesan bishop. The Church prefers to subordinate the diocesan bishop's prerogative to receive dimissorial letters for the ordination of a religious rather than to allow a candidate to be promoted outside of his own rite. Hence, when the diocesan bishop and the religious candidate are of different rites, the religious superior has a legitimate reason for addressing the letters to a bishop of the candidate's rite.

The difference must exist between the rites of the diocesan bishop and the candidate. The diocesan bishop is he in whose territory is located the religious house to which the candidate belongs. If two or more jurisdictions overlap in the same territory, he is to be considered the bishop of the diocese who exercises jurisdiction over the monastery, in so far as the privilege of exemption allows this. Since the proper minister for the ordination of

---

[241] C. 11, X, *de temporibus ordinationum et qualitate ordinandorum,* I, 11; Potthast, n. 1056.

[242] Const. "*Presbyteri graeci,*" 31 aug. 1595, § 4-7—*Bull. Rom. Taur.*, X, 213-214.

[243] Const. "*Sol iustitiae,*" 14 sept. 1739, § 1—*Bull. Rom. Taur.*, XXIV, 580.

[244] Const. "*Etsi pastoralis,*" 26 maii 1742, § VII, xx—*Fontes,* n. 328.

[245] Gasparri, *De Sacra Ordinatione,* n. 929.

an exempt religious is determined by the latter's membership in a definite house, it is the bishop of the diocese in which that house is located who prepares the declaration that his rite differs from that of the candidate.

In the United States, this situation arises when Greek-Ruthenian candidates are members of Latin rite communities. Since the religious house, inasmuch as it is of the Latin rite, is located in a diocese under the rule of a Latin bishop, the latter is determined by law as the proper minister to receive the dimissorial letters for the ordination of the members of that house. Whenever the candidates are of the Greek-Ruthenian rite, however, this bishop is not allowed the exercise of this rite because of the difference in rite. He must yield to the facts of the case by issuing a declaration of this difference.[246]

While by common law the superior may direct the dimissorial letters to any bishop of the candidate's rite, he is restricted by the special provisions made for the Greek-Ruthenians in the United States. Two ordinariates have been established here for the care of the faithful of that rite, a division of jurisdiction being made according to the country of ancestral origin of the faithful.[247] Hence, while the religious superior may not present the candidate to the Latin diocesan bishop, but obtains from him the declaration of difference in rite, he would show contempt for the pontiff's solicitude were he to direct dimissorial letters for the ordination of the Greek-Ruthenian candidate to another than the Greek-Ruthenian bishop appointed to care for the faithful of that rite in the United States. On the other hand, a superior who would send a candidate of the Greek-Ruthenian rite to some bishop other than the one appointed for the faithful of that rite in the United States would not be held liable to the penalty of canon 2410, as if he had violated the right of the diocesan bishop.[248]

---

[246] Canon 966, § 2.

[247] S. C. pro Eccl. Or., decr. 1 mart. 1929, art. 2, 12—*AAS,* XXI (1929), 152; decr. 23 nov. 1940—*AAS,* XXXIII (1941), 27.

[248] The situation is somewhat parallel to that of the Italo-Greeks under the jurisdiction of Latin ordinaries, whose clergy were to be ordained by the Greek bishop assigned for that task. Cf. Benedictus XIV, const. *"Etsi pastoralis,"* 26 maii 1742, VII, viii, xvi-xvii; IX, xix—*Fontes,* n. 328.

The exclusive right of the diocesan bishop to receive dimissorial letters for the ordination of religious attached to houses in his diocese yields to the prohibition against the interchange of rites in ordinations. If, however, this preference is deprived of its force, it seems only proper that the right of the diocesan bishop should be respected. In other words, if it becomes possible for the religious candidate to be ordained by the diocesan bishop, even though there be a difference of rites, the candidate should be presented to him for ordination rather than to another bishop. For then the reason for not approaching the diocesan bishop has creased.

The preference enjoyed by the law of rites can be deprived of its pretension in several ways. A bishop need not ordain the candidate himself, but he may perform it through a substitute, without losing his right to receive the dimissorial letters. If the minister whom he provides is of the same rite as the candidate, all other conditions being satisfied, the superior seems bound to present dimissorial letters for the promotion of the candidate to the diocesan bishop. For though the latter is acting, as he is permitted to do, through another, still the candidate is being promoted by a minister of his own rite. Hence, in that given case, the superior cannot invoke any excuse to justify his directing of the dimissorial letters to another bishop.

For similar reasons, if the diocesan bishop has the necessary permission to promote candidates of another rite,[240] or if the religious has a similar indult to be promoted in another rite, the cause for approaching some other than the diocesan bishop ceases. For in those cases the diocesan bishop can exercise his right without any violation of the ritual law.

It should be noted that canon 966, § 1, makes no reference directly to members of the Oriental rites, but more generally makes its exception applicable to any and every differences of rite. For that reason it is applicable to cases in which the diocesan bishop belongs to an Oriental rite and dimissorial letters for Latin rite candidates are to be issued to a Latin rite bishop after the diocesan bishop has issued the necessary declaration.

---

[240] Petrani, *De Relatione Iuridica inter Diversos Ritus in Ecclesia Catholica* (Romae: Marietti, 1930), p. 95.

3. Absence of the Bishop

The absence of the diocesan bishop is the oldest of the excusing causes. Pope Leo X (1513-1521), although he required Regulars to receive their ordination at the hands of the diocesan bishop, allowed them to approach some other bishop when the diocesan bishop was absent.[250] Although Pope Gregory XIII (1572-1585) did not allow this exception when he revoked the privileges of Regulars to receive orders from any bishop whatsoever and required them to observe the Tridentine norm,[251] it was allowed, first in a particular case,[252] and then through the Clementine decree.[253] Pope Benedict XIV (1740-1758) recognized the diocesan bishop's absence as one of the two excusing causes.[254]

The postulated absence supposes that the diocesan bishop is beyond the confines of the diocese,[255] not merely away from the episcopal city.[256] It matters not whether the reason that occasions this absence is legitimate or otherwise,[257] or of short duration, or that it will not extend through the next stated time for ordinations.[258]

With the exception of Coronata, none of the canonists consulted gave any indication whether the absence must occur at the time the dimissorial letters are being prepared, or whether the absence must concur with the time for the ordinations. If the latter alternative is insisted upon, the situation resolves itself into the fact that the bishop is not holding ordinations, even though provisions have been made to have another bishop ordain in his stead.[259] Hence

---

[250] Const. *"Dum intra,"* 19 dec. 1516, § 11—*Fontes,* n. 72.

[251] Const. *"In tanta rerum,"* 1 mart. 1573—*Bull. Rom. Taur.*, VIII, 39-41.

[252] S. C. C., *Hispanarum,* mense sept. 1589—*Fontes,* n. 2216.

[253] S. C. C., decr. 15 mart. 1596—*Fontes,* n. 2294.

[254] Const. *"Impositi Nobis,"* 27 febr. 1747, § 12—*Fontes,* n. 376.

[255] Benedictus XIV, const. *"Impositi Nobis,"* 27 febr. 1747, § 12—*Fontes,* n. 376.

[256] S. C. C., *Caputaquen.,* 28 ian., 11 febr. 1708, ad I—*Fontes,* n. 3060; cf. Many, *De Sacra Ordinatione,* n. 159; Gasparri, *De Sacra Ordinatione,* n. 922.

[257] Blat, *Commentarium Textus Codicis Iuris Canonici,* III, i, n. 314.

[258] Coronata, *De Sacramentis,* II, n. 45.

[259] Gasparri, *De Sacra Ordinatione,* n. 922; Many, *De Sacra Ordinatione,* n. 159; Coronata, *De Sacramentis,* II, n. 45.

there would be no need to insist on the bishop's absence as a separate cause.

The text of canon 966, § 1, favors the interpretation that the bishop's absence at the time when the dimissorial letters are being prepared suffices as an excusing cause. For the canon deals with the granting of the dimissorial letters, and not with the ordination itself. Since the present tense is used both for the verb *potest* and the dependent verb *sit absens,* it seems that these two times are to be accepted as contemporaneous. On the other hand, in indicating the next reason, viz., the non-holding of ordinations at the next designated date, the future participle is used. Since the law is to be interpreted from its text and context,[260] it appears quite definite that the absence of the bishop at the time the dimissorial letters are being granted is the solely relevant fact.

Certainly the bishop's right to receive the dimissorial letters is protected by canon 2410. Should the superior fraudulently delay the preparation of the letters until the diocesan bishop is absent, and then seize upon the occasion as a means of eluding whatever demand the bishop's rightful claim could make, he would act contrary to canon 967, and be liable to the penalty enacted in canon 2410.

4. Refusal to Hold Ordinations on the Next of the "Six Saturdays"

Should the diocesan bishop intend not to hold ordinations on the next of the "six Saturdays" enumerated by canon 1006, § 2,[261] religious superiors may direct the dimissorial letters to another bishop. This cause originated as a general exception in the Clementine decree, which allowed another bishop to be approached when the diocesan bishop was not holding ordinations.[262] This law did not specify the days on which the bishop was to forfeit his right by not holding ordinations. Hallier (1595-1659) noted that it was the practice in some dioceses to announce by means of an edict

[260] Canon 18.

[261] The four Saturdays in the Ember weeks, the Saturday before Passion Sunday (*Sitientes*) and Holy Saturday.

[262] S. C. C., decr. 15 mart. 1596—*Fontes,* n. 2294.

the fact that the bishop intended to hold ordinations.[263] Monacelli (+ 1715) reproduced a suggested form of such an edict.[264] Pope Innocent XIII (1721-1724)[265] and Pope Benedict XIII (1724-1730)[266] required that the bishops of Spain should give one month's notice before they intended to hold an ordination. If they did not, Regulars knew that the bishop was not ordaining, and were therefore free to approach another bishop.

Canonists, at any rate, maintained that unless an edict had been published to the effect that the bishop intended to hold an ordination, Regulars were free to approach another bishop, even though the diocesan bishop perchance was conducting an ordination for a few persons.[267]

Meanwhile Pope Benedict XIV, in his Constitution *Impositi Nobis,* specified that a bishop was said not to be ordaining if he did not ordain at the next time specified by law for the holding of ordinations,[268] viz., the "six Saturdays" as they are now known.[269] Because of other legislation introduced by this pontiff to effect the proof of the existence of the excusing cause,[270] an edict was no longer necessary, for the religious superior had to establish the fact by means of an official document from the bishop's curia, that

---

[263] *De Sacris Electionibus,* Pars I, Sect. I, Cap. II, art. 4, n. 1. Perhaps this was done for the sake of allowing the candidates to comply with the obligation of having their names announced in the parish church, and of passing the required examination. Cf. Conc. Trident., sess. XXIII, *de ref.,* c. 5, 7. Regulars, however, were declared not bound by the former requirement. Cf. S. C. C., *Mileten.,* 27 apr. 1595—*Fontes,* n. 2285.

[264] *Formularium Legale Practicum Fori Ecclesiastici,* I, tit. iii, formula xxiii.

[265] Const. *"Apostolici muneris,"* 23 maii 1723, § 17—*Fontes,* n. 280.

[266] Const. *"In supremo,"* 23 sept. 1724, § 14—*Fontes,* n. 283.

[267] Passerinus, *De Hominum Statibus et Officiis,* Q. CLXXXIX, art. x, n. 815; Petra, *Commentaria ad Constitutiones Apostolicas,* in const. III (*Sacrosancte*) Benedicti IX, n. 18; Riganti, *Commentaria in Regulas, Constitutiones, et Ordinationes Cancellariae Apostolicae,* Regula XXIV, § III, n. 275; Honorante, *Praxis Secretariae Tribunalis Cardinalis Urbis Vicarii,* C. XII, not. 2.

[268] 27 febr. 1747, § 12—*Fontes,* n. 376.

[269] Cf. c. 7, D. LXXV; c. 2, 3, X, *de temporibus ordinationum et qualitate ordinandorum,* I, 11; Conc. Trident., sess. XXIII, *de ref.,* c. 8.

[270] *Infra,* p. 117.

the bishop was not ordaining on the next day appointed by law. Nevertheless canonists continued to maintain, usually by reference to former authors, that the bishop of necessity was to hold a general ordination; otherwise Regulars were free to approach another bishop.[271] Yet this assertion was not unanimous, and some canonists insisted that, even when the bishop held an ordination for a few, he could not be regarded as failing to hold ordinations, and, consequently, religious could not approach another minister.[272]

Although the Code does not make any requirement regarding the point whether the ordination must be public before it can be stated that the bishop is holding ordinations, canonists, by following the pre-Code interpretation, continue to insist that the ordination be a general one.[273] However, a further difficulty arises from the fact that the expression "general ordinations" is used in two senses, viz., to describe such as are held on the "six Saturdays,"[274] and to indicate such ordinations at which all orders are conferred on whosoever is legitimately presented.[275]

If the former sense is preferred, then to insist that a "general ordination" alone suffices for a bishop to be able to say that he is holding ordinations is the same as describing ordinations which take place on the "six Saturdays." If the latter interpretation is preferred, it amounts to a public ordination, and this seems to be the sense intended by pre-Code authors, as Gasparri, who insisted that the bishop, if it was to be said that he was holding an ordination, had indeed to hold a general ordination at the next legally appointed time.[276]

As long as the historical problem remains in doubt, the interpretation of the present law will likewise receive various interpreta-

---

[271] Gasparri, *De Sacra Ordinatione*, n. 922; Wernz, *Ius Decretalium*, II, i, n. 28.

[272] Many, *De Sacra Ordinatione*, n. 159; Piat, *Praelectiones Iuris Regularis* (3. ed., 3 vols., Tornaci, 1905), II, Q. 355.

[273] Wernz-Vidal, *Ius Canonicum*, IV, i, n. 197; Coronata, *De Sacramentis*, II, n. 45.

[274] Beste, *Introductio*, p. 547; Vermeersch-Creusen, *Epitome*, II, n. 270.

[275] Cappello, *De Sacra Ordinatione*, n. 568; Regatillo, *Ius Sacramentarium*, II, n. 161.

[276] *De Sacra Ordinatione*, n. 922.

tions. The text of canon 966, § 1, does not require that the bishop fail to hold a general ordination. Coronata suggests the practical remedy that, if the bishop is holding a private ordination, but is unwilling on that occasion to ordain the religious candidates, he can grant his permission for the religious to approach another bishop, as he is allowed to do.[277]

By its reference to canon 1006, § 2, the law restricts the determining occasions to the "six Saturdays" for ordination. Should the bishop fail to ordain on one of these days, even though he legitimately transfers the ordination date to a Sunday or some other day, whether this be done in virtue of the concession made in canon 1006, § 3, or of a special indult, the religious superior is not bound to direct dimissorial letters to him on such an occasion, but may approach another bishop.[278]

A bishop is considered as holding ordinations even though he employs the service of another minister in his stead.[279] In such a case, however, he must be present within the confines of the diocese; for if he is absent, he is considered as not holding ordinations, even though actually another ministers for him. But, whether present or absent from the diocese, if the ordinations are performed by an auxiliary or coadjutor bishop, he is considered as holding ordinations.[280] Likewise, if the ordinations are held in another part of the diocese than the episcopal city, the bishop must be considered as fulfilling his obligation of holding an ordination, and on such occasions religious may not be presented to another bishop with that as an excuse.[281]

Should the religious institute enjoy a privilege to receive orders outside of the usual days for ordination, and should the bishop refuse to ordain the candidates presented by the superior on those

---

[277] *De Sacramentis*, II, n. 45.

[278] Augustine, *Commentary*, IV, 441; Coronata, *De Sacramentis*, II, n. 45; O'Brien, *The Exemption of Religious in Church Law*, p. 189.

[279] Gasparri, *De Sacra Ordinatione*, n. 922; Many, *De Sacra Ordinatione*, n. 159; Coronata, *De Sacramentis*, II, n. 45; Augustine, *Commentary*, IV, 441.

[280] Passerinus, *De Hominum Statibus et Officiis*, Q. CLXXXIX, art. x, n. 814; Piat, *Praelectiones Iuris Regularis*, II, Q. 353.

[281] S. C. C., *Caputaquen.*, 28 ian., 11 febr. 1708, ad I—*Fontes*, n. 3060; Coronata, *De Sacramentis*, II, n. 45.

days, this cannot be used as a pretext for approaching another bishop.[282] It is only the refusal of the bishop to ordain on the next day designated by law that allows religious to approach another minister.[283]

5. Vacancy of the Diocese

When the diocese is vacant and the prelate who governs it does not have espiscopal consecration, the religious superior may direct the dimissorials to any other bishop.[284] The occasion of the vacancy of the diocese does not actually involve the diocesan bishop, since, as is evident, there is no diocesan bishop. Consequently this exception was not treated in the Clementine decree nor in the Constitution *Impositi Nobis,* since those documents treated strictly of the rights of the diocesan bishop. However, the jurisprudence of the Sacred Congregations recognized that, when the diocesan see was vacant, religious might be sent to any bishop for ordination.[285] While pre-Code law allowed the religious superior to direct the dimissorial letters to any bishop during the vacancy of the diocesan see, this is now allowed only when the prelate who governs the diocese does not himself possess episcopal consecration.

An episcopal see becomes vacant at the death of the bishop, at the acceptance of his resignation by the Holy Father, or when the bishop has received notice of his transfer or removal.[286] While the task of electing a vicar capitular or a diocesan administrator devolves upon the cathedral chapter or the diocesan consultors,[287] it may be noted that the diocesan bishop, though appointed to another see, retains the rule of his former diocese with the powers

[282] Benedictus XIV, const. "*Impositi Nobis,*" 27 febr. 1747, § 15—*Fontes,* n. 376.

[283] S. C. C., *Lunen.-Sarzanen.,* 18 aug. 1888—*Fontes,* n. 4273. Cf. S. C. Ep. et Reg., *Castren.,* 18 iul. 1732—*Fontes,* 1850. A different interpretation was given in S. C. C., *Caputaquen.,* 6 iul. 1709—Pallottini, s.v. *Sacramentum Ordinis,* II, n. 8.

[284] Canon 966, § 1.

[285] S. C. C., 3 iun. 1599—*Fontes,* n. 2325; S. C. C., decr. 24 aug. 1619—*Fontes,* n. 2418; S. C. C., *Tirasonen.,* 11 maii, 8 iun., 13 iul. 1782—*Fontes,* n. 3823.

[286] Canon 430, § 1.

[287] Canons 431; 432; 423; 427.

of a vicar capitular and the honorary privileges of a residential bishop.[288] Likewise a vicar or prefect apostolic, even though his term of assignment has expired, retains full control of the diocese until his successor assumes government.[289]

Should the prelate who rules the vacant diocese have the necessary power of orders, but if one of the four exceptions already considered occurs, the religious superiors can approach another minister as if the situation had occurred with a bishop. Thus, should the vicar capitular give his permission, be absent from the diocese, not hold ordinations, or be of a different rite than the candidate, the dimissorial letters may be addressed to another bishop.[290]

When the governing prelate of the vacant diocese does not have episcopal consecration, but nevertheless enjoys some power of orders, Vermeersch (1858-1936) seemed to oblige religious to approach him for ordination in so far as he can confer the orders for which the dimissorials are being issued.[291]

B. *Proof of the Existence of the Excuse*

In each instance in which there is present any one of the five excusing occasions on which a religious superior is permitted to address the dimissorial letters to a bishop other than the diocesan bishop, the fact must be evident to the ordaining prelate from an authentic testimonial of the diocesan bishop's curia.[292]

According to the Clementine decree, the religious superior was obliged to express in the dimissorial letters the reason why the diocesan bishop was not ordaining, viz., his absence or his failure to hold ordinations.[293] The manner of ascertaining the existence of this reason was not indicated, but it probably could have been learned from the edict which the bishops in some places used to publish regarding the time when ordinations would be held.[294] It

---

[288] Canon 430, § 3.

[289] Canon 311.

[290] Coronata, *De Sacramentis,* II, n. 45; Augustine, *Commentary,* IV, 441.

[291] *Epitome,* II, n. 241.

[292] Canon 966, § 2.

[293] S. C. C., decr. 15 mart. 1596—*Fontes,* n. 2294.

[294] *Supra,* pp. 91-92.

was also the custom, in some places, to furnish this information in the form of an authentic letter from the diocesan curia, even before the practice became general law.[295] The Constitution *Impositi Nobis* made such an authentic document from the diocesan curia, as signed by the vicar general, the chancellor, or the bishop's secretary, a condition for the validity of the dimissorial letters addressed to another bishop.[296]

While the pre-Code law required this attestation to be furnished only when the dimissorial letters were sent to another bishop because of the diocesan bishop's absence or failure to hold ordinations at the appointed times, the present law clearly indicates that the authentic attestation must be furnished in each instance, *singulis in casibus.*[297] The burden of requesting such a testimonial will normally fall on the religious superior who prepares the letters. It is to be prepared by the diocesan bishop's curia, and is to bear the usual signs of authenticity, viz., the signature of a competent curial official, and normally also the chancery seal.[298]

While this authentic document, or at least a duly notarized copy, is to accompany the dimissorial letters, it does not seem required for the validity of these letters. For that provision has not been retained from the Constitution *Impositi Nobis,* and, according to canon 6, 6°, should be considered as having lost its obligation. Likewise, canon 966, § 2, does not indicate that the curial attestation is a requirement that is essential for the validity of the dimissorials. Since such conditions must be definitely indicated, but are in fact not indicated thus in the present law, the testimonial which certifies the existence of one of the excusing occasions does not seem required for the validity of the dimissorial letters.[299] Nevertheless, unless the ordaining bishop has this legitimate proof of the existence of the excusing circumstance, he is liable to the same penalty as if he ordained without possessing the needed dimissorial letters.[300]

[295] Benedictus XIV, *Institutiones Ecclesiasticae,* XXIII.

[296] Benedictus XIV, 27 febr. 1747, § 12—*Fontes,* n. 376.

[297] Canon 966, § 2. Cf. Gasparri, *De Sacra Ordinatione,* n. 923.

[298] Augustine, *Commentary,* IV, 442; Blat, *Commentarium Textus Codicis Iuris Canonici,* III, i, n. 314.

[299] Canon 11.

[300] Canon 2373, 1°, 4°.

CHAPTER V

The Ordination

While the rite of ordination of an exempt religious is essentially the same as that for a secular candidate, some of the details deserve attention because of the modifications involved.

ARTICLE I. THE CEREMONIES OF ORDINATION

Two variations occur in the ceremonies of ordination when a Regular is being promoted. In the ordination to the subdiaconate, after the candidates have been assembled before the bishop, he ordinarily would read the admonition *Filii dilectissimi,* which treats of the gravity of the obligations they are to assume. The rubrics direct, however, that if all the candidates are religious, this admonition is omitted.[1] However, the term *religiosi* is in this instance to be understood as designating Regulars exclusively, that is, such as have already made solemn profession.[2] For these candidates have already assumed some of the clerical obligations which begin to oblige seculars with the subdiaconate, viz., the personal obligation of reciting the canonical hours[3] and the inability to contract a valid marriage.[4]

Another variation occurs at the conclusion of the ceremonies for the conferral of the priesthood. At that time Regulars make a promise of obedience, not to the bishop,[5] but into the hands of the minister for the Regular prelate.[6]

---

[1] Pontificale Rom., tit. *De ordinibus conferendis.*

[2] Nabuco, *Pontificalis Romani Expositio Juridico-Practica* (3 vols., Petropoli: Editôra Vozes Ltda., 1945), I, n. 108; de Antoñana, "Consultationes"—*CpR,* V (1924), 226-228.

[3] Canon 610, § 3.

[4] Canon 1073.

[5] S. C. C., dubium 2 maii 1676—Pallottini, s.v. "Sacramentum Ordinis," III, n. 49.

[6] Pontificale Rom., tit. *De ordinibus conferendis.*

ARTICLE II. THE TIME OF ORDINATION

While the present law allows the bishop, for a grave reason, to confer sacred orders on Sundays and on holy days of obligation,[7] some religious institutes, and especially Regulars, enjoy the privilege to receive orders *extra tempora.* Thus Regulars may receive sacred orders on any Sunday or feast day, even though this is now a suppressed feast.[8] The principal value of these privileges, which would approximate the faculties granted to all bishops if the suppressed feasts are excluded, is that the bishop does not require a grave cause to ordain Regulars on such days, but he can do so for any just cause.[9] Should the bishop enjoy a special indult to ordain on other days, he can also use this in favor of religious candidates.

ARTICLE III. THE PLACE OF ORDINATION

Ordinarily the minister will decide the place of ordination, which, for a just cause, can be the church or oratory attached to the religious house.[10] Since the conferring of orders is a pontifical function,[11] the minister is further restricted by the limitations imposed on his use of the pontifical insignia, viz., the crosier and miter.[12] Tonsure and the minor orders, when conferred outside of Holy Mass, do not require the use of the pontifical insignia.[13]

---

[7] Canon 1006, § 3. Excluded, however, are such feast days as have been suppressed in the universal Church. Cf. P.C.I., 15 maii 1936—*AAS,* XXVIII (1936), 210. If the feast remains in the universal calendar, but is not of obligation in that country, it seems that major orders may be conferred on such days. Cf. Apostolic Delegate, letter, May 13, 1938—Bouscaren, *The Canon Law Digest,* II, 248-249.

[8] Coronata, *De Sacramentis,* II, n. 240; Cappello, *De Sacra Ordinatione,* n. 564. Capobianco (*Privilegia et Facultates Ordinis Fratrum Minorum,* n. 130-131) prefers not to extend the privileges to the suppressed feasts.

[9] Ledwolorz, "De Regularium Privilegiis Recipiendi Sacros Ordines extra Tempora et Non Servatis Interstitiis"—*Antonianum,* XX (1945), 427-432.

[10] Canon 1009, § 2.

[11] S. C. C., *Monopolitana,* 9 febr. 1924—*AAS,* XVII (1925), 245.

[12] Canon 337, § 2.

[13] Beste, *Introductio,* p. 547; Nabuco, *Pontificalis Romani Expositio Juridico-Practica,* I, n. 70; Coronata, *De Sacramentis,* II, n. 242.

Therefore, whenever any prelate confers these orders without the use of a crosier and miter, he may perform the ordination without first obtaining the permission of the local ordinary.[14]

Cardinals may pontificate anywhere in the world,[15] except that they must apprise the ordinary if the Church is a cathedral, and they are subject also to certain limitations within the city of Rome.[16] Legates of the Holy Father, if they are bishops,[17] and also metropolitans[18] may use the pontifical insignia within their respective jurisdictions, except in the cathedral churches, unless the ordinary has been notified. However, they would be required to obtain the local ordinary's permission to perform an ordination, since the Legates are allowed the use of pontificals for the celebration of the divine offices, while the metropolitans may not perform those pontifical functions if they evince and connote the possession of jurisdiction. Bishops may pontificate anywhere within their diocese, even in churches subject to exempt religious. Outside of their territory, they must first obtain the express, or at least have reasonably presumed, permission from the local ordinary, and, if it be an exempt church, also from the religious superior.[19] Since vicars and prefects apostolic, as well as abbots and prelates *nullius,* cannot validly ordain outside of their territories,[20] unless they have the power to ordain from another title, there is no need to consider their use of the faculty to ordain in another's territory. A Regular abbot *de regimine,* after he has received the abbatial blessing, has the power to ordain and a right to the use of pontificals.[21] Since Regular abbots do not have a territory entrusted to their care, the constant jurisprudence of the Sacred Congregation of Sacred Rites has been to allow them the use of pontifical insignia and the performance of pontifical functions in their own churches, that is, in such as are attached to or

---

[14] Canon 1008.

[15] Canon 239, § 1, 15°.

[16] Canons 240, § 3; 823, § 3. Cf. S. C. Caeremonial., decr. 2 dec. 1930—*AAS,* XXIII (1931), 56-59.

[17] Canon 269, § 3.

[18] Canon 274, 6°.

[19] Canon 337, § 1.

[20] Canon 957, § 2.

[21] Canons 625; 325.

incorporated with the monastery they rule.[22] Unless the abbot enjoys a special indult, he cannot pontificate outside of these churches even with the permission of the local ordinary.[23] Augustine (1872-1943) maintained, however, that in the United States and Switzerland there exists a contrary custom, which permits abbots to pontificate in other than their own churches, if they be invited to do so.[24] Should the abbot enjoy an indult to pontificate in other than his own churches, he may not make use of this faculty without the express permission of the bishop.[25] Such permission seems necessary too if the abbot pontificates outside of his own churches in virtue of an existing acknowledged custom.[26] It is permissible, however, for an abbot to permit another of the same order to pontificate in his churches.[27] The place where the abbot confers tonsure and minor orders is not, however, expressed as a condition for the validity of the ordination.

While the Code seems to require permission of both the local ordinary and the religious superior when a visitor pontificates in an exempt church,[28] some authors maintain that the permission of the superior of such a church is sufficient.[29] Whatever may be the value of the latter interpretation for other pontifical acts, it

[22] *Pampilonen.*, 8 maii 1617—*Decr. Auth.*, n. 351; *Brixien.*, 28 iun. 1642—*Decr. Auth.*, n. 803; *decr.* 27 sept. 1659, ad 19—*Decr. Auth.*, n. 1131; *Bononien.*, 5 iul. 1698—*Decr. Auth.*, n. 2000; ep. 31 mart. 1744—*Decr. Auth.*, n. 2376; decr. 27 aug. 1822, ad 2, 3—*Decr. Auth.*, n. 2624; *Bahien. in Brasilia*, 23 maii 1846, ad 3—*Decr. Auth.*, n. 2907; *Liverpolitana*, 13 iun. 1902—*Decr. Auth.*, n. 4098. Cf. (Anonymous), "Use of Pontificals by Benedictine Abbots" —*ER*, CVIII (1943), 454-456.

[23] S. R. C., *Tornacen.*, 2 aug. 1631—*Decr. Auth.*, n. 577; *Barcionen.*, 11 iul. 1739—*Decr. Auth.*, n. 2348; *Liverpolitana*, 13 iun. 1902—*Decr. Auth.*, n. 4098. Beste, *Introductio*, p. 429.

[24] *Rights and Duties of Ordinaries according to the Code and Apostolic Faculties* (St. Louis, Mo., 1924), pp. 38-39.

[25] S. R. C., *Ordinis Monachorum Sancti Basilii*, 18 dec. 1846—*Decr. Auth.*, n. 2923. For such an indult, cf. S. R. C., *Goritien.*, 11, 18 aug. 1770—*Decr. Auth.*, n. 2488.

[26] Beste, *Introductio*, p. 429.

[27] S. R. C., *Fesulana*, 1 oct. 1710, ad 3—*Decr. Auth.*, n. 2080; *Liverpolitana*, 12 iun. 1902—*Decr. Auth.*, n. 4098.

[28] Canon 337, § 1; Vermeersch-Creusen, *Epitome*, I, n. 453; Coronata, *Institutiones*, I, n. 394.

[29] Regatillo, *Institutiones Iuris Canonici* (2 vols., Santander: Sal Terrae, 1941-1942), I, n. 486; Augustine, *Commentary*, II, 357.

does not seem applicable to the more specific ruling of canon 1008, which reserves the right to perform ordinations in which pontifical insignia are used to the local ordinary, whose permission must first be obtained.[80]

When the religious superior enjoys the necessary power of orders and wishes to promote his own subjects for whom he can issue the dimissorial letters, he does not need the permission of the local ordinary to use his right to ordain.[81] If, however, pontifical insignia are to be used at the ordination, he seems necessarily to have a right to use these in the place, either in virtue of a grant made by the law, as it is made to cardinals everywhere in the world,[82] to bishops in their own diocese,[83] and to Regular abbots *de regimine* in their own churches,[84] or in consequence of a permission granted by the local ordinary.[85] For the right to ordain is distinct from the right to use pontificals.[86] Thus a religious superior who is a titular bishop requires the permission of the local ordinary, not with a view to the conferring of orders, but because use is made of the miter and crosier in the conferring of orders.

ARTICLE IV. RECORDS AND DOCUMENTS

After the ordination, the names of those who have been promoted to orders, as well as that of the minister, together with the place and date of the ordination, are to be recorded in a special book kept for this purpose at the chancery of the place of the ordination.[87] In this book is to be kept the information on all who have

[80] S. C. C., *Bisinianen.*, a. 1573—*Fontes*, n. 2119; *Civitatis Regalis in Indiis* (*Limana*), mense febr. 1586, ad 30—*Fontes*, n. 2152; *Neapolitana*, 27 febr. 1649—*Fontes*, n. 2694.

[81] *Supra*, pp. 66-68.

[82] Canon 239, § 1, 15°.

[83] Canon 337, § 1.

[84] *Supra*, pp. 120-121. Cf. S. R. C., *Liverpolitana*, 13 iun. 1902—*Decr. Auth.*, n. 4098, in which it is clearly stated that the permission of the local ordinary is not required for an abbot to pontificate in his own church.

[85] Canon 1008.

[86] Goyeneche, "Consultationes"—*CpR*, V (1924), 164-165. This was already held by Gasparri (*De Sacra Ordinatione*, nn. 92-97, 918). Cf. (Anonymous), "De Ordinatione a Proprio Superiore Religioso"—*Periodica*, XII (1924), (163)-(164).

[87] Canon 1010, § 1; Nabuco, *op. cit.*, I, n. 68.

been ordained in the territory, whether or not they belong to the diocese.[38] Included, therefore, are religious who have been promoted with dimissorial letters from their superiors.

The Code does not indicate clearly that the records of religious who have been promoted by their superior must be forwarded to the diocesan chancery for entry into this central record.[39] It seems a desirable practice, however, that the central record be maintained as a permanent and complete listing for all who have been promoted within the confines of the diocese. The individual files of reports, dispensations, attestations, etc., however, should remain in the curia of the religious institute, since this information furnished the basis for the preparation of the dimissorial letters.

Those who have been ordained are to be given an authentic attestation of their ordination.[40] From the general nature of this canon, it appears proper that just as the bishop is to furnish such a document to all he has promoted, even though they be his own subjects, so too when the religious superior has ordained he should present those ordained with such an authentic attestation.

When promotion to orders has taken place at the hands of a bishop other than the candidate's ordinary, this document serves as official information for the superior, from which will be prepared the official book of ordinations kept in the religious curia.[41]

The religious superior has the further obligation of sending official notice to the pastor at the place of baptism that the religious has been promoted to the subdiaconate.[42] Such notification must be sent even though, in the case of a Regular, a similar notice was transmitted at the time of his solemn profession.[43] For there are involved two separate laws, and also two distinct impediments should marriage ever be attempted.[44]

---

[38] Coronata, *De Sacramentis,* II, n. 246.

[39] Augustine (*Commentary,* IV, 548-549) directed that the records be kept at the actual place of ordination, that is, at the abbey church.

[40] Canon 1010, § 2.

[41] Canon 1010, § 2.

[42] Canon 1011.

[43] Cf. canon 576, § 2.

[44] Schaefer, *De Religiosis,* n. 458; Goyeneche, "Consultationes"—*CpR,* I (1920), 227-228. Cf. canon 1072; 1073.

CHAPTER VI

Delicts in the Ordination of Exempt Religious

The discipline established by the Church provides for the public good and order. In the administration of orders, the Church seeks through its laws to protect not only the clerical state, but also the rights of the several persons who participate in each ordination. Specifically, concern is shown for the rights of the candidate, of the religious superior, and of the minister of the sacrament. To guarantee its laws against transgression, the Church further establishes penalties, both to deter the innocent from committing the crime and to reform and punish the guilty.

The discussion at this time will be concerned with the material element of the several penal laws. It is presumed that the norms on imputability[1] and the doctrine on co-operators[2] will be applied in each case.

ARTICLE I. DELICTS IN THE ACCEPTANCE OF CANDIDATES

The Church protects its right to worthy ministers and the candidate's right freely to seek his state of life by forbidding that anyone, in any manner or for any reason, be forced into the clerical state, or that a canonically suitable candidate be turned away.[3] Regardless of his dignity, anyone who forces a man to enter either the clerical state, or the religious life, or to make a religious profession, is by that very act excommunicated with a non-reserved censure.[4]

It is quite obvious that the penalty is incurred only if the candidate is forced to enter the clerical state or the religious life, and not if a suitable aspirant was turned away. Even in the latter case, however, the offender is guilty of a grave injustice both to society and to the candidate.

---

1 Canons 2199-2211; 2228-2229.

2 Canons 2209; 2231.

3 Canon 971.

4 Canon 2352.

The use of force deprives the candidate of his right to choose freely a state of life. Besides exposing the sacrament of orders to nullity, and occasioning possible consequent damage to the faithful, force frequently results in dissatisfied ministers who fail to show the zeal and attention demanded by their vocation, if they do not actually desert the clerical state with scandal to the faithful. Precisely to exclude the possibility of force, the candidate, before ordination, testifies under oath to his freedom in embracing the clerical state and its obligations.[5]

In regard to candidates for the priesthood in the religious life, the prohibition of canon 2352 may become operative at four points of time: at the reception into the novitiate, at the temporal profession, at the perpetual profession, and at the reception of tonsure. Since the entrance into the novitiate is strictly the entrance into religion, any force exerted before that time, as at the time of the postulancy, would not result in the censure.[6] If force is used with a view to compelling the candidate to make profession, either temporary or perpetual, the person guilty of such coercion is liable to the penalty. Inasmuch as the clerical state is entered with the reception of tonsure, the use of force at that time also is punished with the incurring of a censure, not however, for the other orders.[7]

The entrance into the novitiate, the profession of vows, and the reception of tonsure, if the censure is to be incurred, must be the result of the force employed. Should the force exerted be ineffective in producing the results, or should the compulsion have ceased and the originally intended results nevertheless occur, but of the candidate's own free will, then the censure is not incurred.[8]

That is considered a sufficient force which, when applied to a reluctant will, prevails upon it to act. The manner in which compulsion is applied, as through violence or grave fear, whether it be exerted directly or indirectly, as by fraud, deceit, threats, or even

---

[5] *Supra*, pp. 34-35.

[6] Cappello, *Tractatus Canonico-Moralis de Censuris* (3. ed., Romae: Marietti, 1933), n. 419 (hereafter cited *De Censuris*); Augustine, *Commentary*, VIII, 407, footnote 4.

[7] Beste, *Introductio*, p. 979. Cf. canon 108, § 1.

[8] Cappello, *De Censuris*, n. 419.

importune pleadings, is immaterial, provided that the decision to enter religion or the clerical state, or to make profession, results from the force.[9]

The use of force should not be confused with licit and even commendable efforts made by right-minded persons to present to possible candidates the sublimity of the religious life or the clerical state. In fact, priests are urged by the law of the Code to encourage and aid youths who show signs of a clerical vocation.[10]

With the exception of cardinals,[11] the censure can be incurred by anyone, regardless of dignity, who is capable of incurring a censure. The penalty is an excommunication which is not reserved.

The candidate who has been forced into the clerical state of the religious life can obtain either a declaration of nullity or at least a declaration of freedom from the obligations. If the novitiate was entered[12] or if profession was made in consequence of force, grave fear, or fraud, the acts are invalid,[13] and a sentence of nullity can be sought from the competent tribunal. Ordination, however, even though it be received under duress, is valid, unless the requisite intention for its reception was lacking. In the respective case the cleric can request a judgment either of the invalidity of his ordination or of his freedom from the clerical obligations.[14]

Indirectly associated with the ordination of exempt religious is the reception, contrary to the provisions of canon 542, of an unsuitable candidate into the novitiate. For the irregularities and impediments to orders must be considered already at that time. Since there is considerable disagreement among canonists as to the precise interpretation of the requirement that the candidate be free from irregularities and impediments to orders at the time he enters the novitiate,[15] a religious superior who acts in good faith in fol-

---

[9] Wernz-Vidal, *Ius Canonicum,* VII, n. 481; Augustine, *Commentary,* VIII, 407; Beste, *Introductio,* p. 979.

[10] Canon 1353.

[11] Canon 2227, § 2.

[12] Canon 542, 1°.

[13] Canon 572, § 1, 4°.

[14] Canons 211, § 1; 214; 1993-1998. Clerics in minor orders can be reduced to the lay state through their own expressed desire for the reduction. Cf. canon 211, § 2.

[15] *Supra,* pp. 15-17.

lowing at least a probable opinion could advance this in his own defense. For the penalty for a superior who acts in bad faith in this matter is a *ferendae sententiae* penalty, and may extend even to privation from office.[16]

ARTICLE II. DELICTS IN THE ISSUING OF DIMISSORIAL LETTERS

A religious superior who, contrary to the provisions of canons 965-967, presumes to send his subjects to a bishop other than the proper bishop incurs automatically a suspension for one month from the celebration of Holy Mass.[17]

This canon protects the right of the diocesan bishop to receive dimissorial letters for the ordination of exempt religious attached to religious houses located in his diocese. The penalty is incurred when the religious superior issues the dimissorial letters, for precisely in that act the candidates are presented to the ordaining bishop, even though ordination does not follow.[18]

An analysis of canons 965-967 reveals the possibility of three delicts by which a religious superior could offend against the rights of the diocesan bishop and, consequently, incur the penalty of this penal canon: 1) Directing dimissorial letters to some other than the diocesan bishop, who has the right to receive them, in the absence of one of the five reasons listed in canon 966, § 1; 2) Directing dimissorial letters to the bishop of the diocese in which is located the religious house to which the candidate had been fraudently transferred; and 3) Directing letters to a bishop other than the diocesan bishop after the preparation of dimissorial letters has been delayed fraudulently until the diocesan bishop would be absent or would refrain from holding ordinations.[19]

Should one of the causes listed in canon 966, § 1, allow the superior to send the dimissorial letters to some other than the diocesan bishop, it seems that no penalty would be incurred even though the authentic attestation were not presented. For the

[16] Canon 2411.

[17] Canon 2410.

[18] Blat, *Commentarium Textus Codicis Iuris Canonici,* V, n. 256.

[19] Cappello, *De Censuris,* n. 562; Chelodi, *Ius Poenale* (Tridenti, 1925), n. 112.

present law does not repeat the provisions of the pre-Code discipline which required the superior to attach the attestation to the dimissorial letters under threat of their invalidity.[20]

The dimissorial letters must actually be issued if the incurring of the penalty is to result. Thus a superior who has fraudulently transferred the candidate, or delayed the preparation of the dimissorial letters for his ordination, commits the delict only when the letters are sent to some other bishop after such a transfer or delay.

Moreover, the letters granted must be valid dimissorial letters. Hence they must be issued by a superior who is competent to prepare them. Should another, even though a superior, usurp the power, no valid letters exist, and the crime of sending dimissorial letters to the unauthorized minister is not committed.[21] However, the penalty can be incurred, not only by those superiors who have the right to issue dimissorial letters as acknowledged for them in the law.[22] but also by those who enjoy this authority through the possession of a privilege.[23]

Similarly it is postulated that the dimissorial letters be issued on behalf of a subject. If a superior issues them for a religious who is not truly subject to him, he seems not to incur the penalty.

The use of the expression *praesumpserit* indicates that complete malice is required for the incurring of the suspension, which, however, is a vindictive penalty, not a censure. The penalty prohibits the superior from offering Holy Mass for a period of one month.

Two other canons also protect the proper issuing of the dimissorial letters. A rather general law covers some cases not comprehended under canon 2410: The falsifying or forging of ecclesiastical documents is to be punished according to the gravity of the crime.[24] Thus a superior who, without the authority to issue dimissorial letters, nevertheless issues purportedly authentic letters, incurs liability for the delict of forgery in preparing such documents. The penalty for this delict is not specified, but depends on the sentence of a competent judge.

---

[20] *Supra*, p. 117.

[21] Cappello, *De Censuris*, n. 562; Coronata, *Institutiones*, IV, n. 2230.

[22] Canon 964, 2°.

[23] P.C.I., 2-3 iun. 1918—*AAS*, X (1918), 347.

[24] Canon 2362.

A further penal canon is involved in the use of such false dimissorial letters. A candidate who maliciously approaches ordination, either devoid of dimissorial letters or with false ones, or before the canonical age, or after omitting a lower order, is automatically suspended from the order received.[25] This penalty prevents the exercise of the order received and forbids further the reception and exercise of higher orders.[26] It does not affect those orders which have previously been received.[27] Those are false dimissorial letters which have been prepared by a person other than the one to whom they are attributed, or which contain a false statement or assertion, or which have been prepared by someone who has not the power to issue dimissorial letters.[28]

ARTICLE III. DELICTS ON THE PART OF THE MINISTER OF ORDERS

A suspension from conferring orders for one year, reserved to the Holy See, is automatically incurred: 1) by those who ordain, contrary to the provisions of canon 955, the subject of another without the possession of dimissorial letters from that ordinary, and 2) except in the cases of legitimate privilege, by those who ordain a religious who belongs to a religious family located outside of the ordaining minister's territory, even though the candidate has dimissorial letters from his superior, unless it is legitimately proved that one of the causes described in canon 966 has occurred.[29]

Just as canon 2410 imposes a penalty for the unwarranted preparation of dimissorial letters, so canon 2373 establishes a penalty for the conferring of the forbidden ordination. More, it does not only protect the diocesan bishop's right as determined according to canon 965, but also the superior's exclusive prerogative to authorize the ordination of his subjects.

Each candidate for orders is to be ordained by his own bishop or by another who possesses the dimissorial letters issued by him.[30]

---

[25] Canon 2374.

[26] Canon 2279, § 2, 5°.

[27] Cappello, *De Censuris*, n. 550.

[28] Coronata, *Institutiones*, IV, n. 2163.

[29] Canon 2373, 1°, 4°.

[30] Canon 955.

In the case of exempt religious it is ordinarily the major superior who is to issue the dimissorials. At first sight there may be some question of the applicability of canon 955 to religious, since that canon uses the term *Episcopus,* whereas canon 2373 makes reference to the ordinary. Canonists however have adopted the interpretation that a minister who ordains an exempt religious without the possession of the needed dimissorial letters from the candidate's superior is liable to the penalty enacted in canon 2373.[31]

The other provision complements canon 2410 in protecting the diocesan bishop's right to receive dimissorial letters. Exception is made, however, for legitimate privileges which permit the candidate to receive his ordination from someone other than the diocesan bishop, even when one of the five cases described in canon 966, § 1, does not occur.

The obligation of having legitimate proof of the existence of an excusing circumstance is clearly a concern of the ordaining prelate. Unless this evidence is at hand, the minister is liable to the penalty of suspension, for one year, from the conferral of orders.

Through these penal canons the Church strives to maintain the observance of the discipline it has instituted for the preservation of peace and order.

---

[31] Coronata, *Institutiones,* IV, n. 2158; Cappello, *De Censuris,* n. 522; Regatillo, *Ius Sacramentarium,* II, n. 62.

CONCLUSIONS

As a result of this study, the following conclusions are offered:

1. The promotion of religious to orders was consistently accepted and encouraged by the Church.
2. The preparation of a candidate for the priesthood in the religious life should begin before his novitiate.
3. The candidate should be free of all impediments and irregularities which debar his licit ordination before his admission to the novitiate. A sufficiently probable opinion permits acceptance of a candidate with such irregularities and impediments which will certainly cease to debar him from ordination, either because the basis of the irregularity or the impediment will cease, or because a remission of the disqualification will be effected by his own act or with faculties already communicated by law or privilege.
4. Promotion to major orders may not precede final profession, even though an extraneous canonical title can be supplied.
5. Promotion to orders may not take place before the requirements determined by the four factors of the previous making of the religious profession, of the attainment of the chronological age, of the completion of the requisite theological studies, and of the observance of the law of interstices have been satisfied, as required for the particular order.
6. The profession of faith and the oath against modernism are to be made before that local ordinary, or his delegate, in whose territory the ordination takes place.
7. In the present discipline the selection of exempt religious candidates for orders is reserved exclusively to the religious superior.
8. Only that provincial superior can prepare dimissorial letters who truly retains jurisdiction over the candidate and rules the religious house of which the candidate is a member.
9. No provision is made in the present law for determining the proper bishop for the reception of the dimissorial letters with reference to the ordination of a religious who does not belong to any religious house.

10. The religious superior who can prepare the dimissorial letters may, if he enjoys the necessary power of orders, personally ordain the candidate.
11. Consideration of the historical development of the power of Regular abbots *de regimine* to ordain has helped clarify the interpretation of his present faculties.
12. Regular abbots *de regimine* who are priests and have received the abbatial blessing can ordain their subjects validly anywhere. If pontifical insignia are used, the ordination is licit wherever the abbot may use the crosier and miter.
13. The local ordinary, unless he is the ordaining bishop, cannot demand that the exempt religious of his diocese present themselves to him for an examination before ordination.
14. Simple residence is insufficient for determining which bishop has the right to receive the dimissorial letters.
15. Dimissorial letters may be sent to some other than the diocesan bishop if the latter is absent from the diocese at the time the dimissorial letters are prepared, without reference to his presence or absence at the time contemplated for the ordination.
16. When the diocesan bishop ordains on any day other than the "Six Saturdays," exempt religious may approach another bishop for the reception of orders.
17. The attestation of the existence of an excusing cause, as described in canon 966, is not required for the validity of the dimissorial letters. No penalty is incurred by the religious superior when dimissorial letters are sent to some other than the diocesan bishop in the presence of one of these causes even without the attestation.
18. The granting of dimissorial letters, and only this, is postulated for the incurring of the penalty enacted in canon 2410.

APPENDIX

Text of the sworn attestation prescribed for a religious candidate for the priesthood.

Ego subsignatus N. N. alumnus Ordinis vel Congregationis N. N. cum petitionem Superioribus exhibuerim pro recipiendo subdiaconatus ordine, diligenter re perpensa coram Deo, iuramento interposito, testificor:

1. Nulla me coactione, seu vi, aut nullo impelli timore in recipiendo eodem sacro ordine, sed ipsum sponte exoptare, ac plena liberaque voluntate eumdem cum adnexis oneribus amplecti velle.

2. Fateor mihi plene esse cognita cuncta onera ex eodem sacro ordine dimanantia, quae sponte amplector, ac Deo opitulante propono me toto vitae curriculo diligenter servare.

3. Quae castitatis voto ac coelibatus lege praecipiuntur, clare me percipere testor, eaque integre servare usque ad extremum vitae, Deo adiuvante, firmiter statuo.

4. Denique sincera fide spondeo igitur me fore, ad normam sacrorum canonum, obsequentissime obtemperaturum iis omnibus quae mihi a Praepositis, iuxta Ecclesiae disciplinam, praecipientur, paratus, virtutum exempla tum opere, cum sermone, aliis praebere, adeo ut tanti officii susceptione retributionem a Deo promissam accipere merear. Sic testor ac iuro, super haec Sancta Dei Evangelia, quae manu mea tango.

Die . . . Mensis . . . Anni. . . .

____

(Manu propria)

BIBLIOGRAPHY

Sources

Acta Apostolicae Sedis, Romae, 1909-

Acta Ordinis Fratrum Minorum, Ad Claras Aquas, 1882-

Acta Sanctae Sedis, 41 vols., Romae, 1865-1908.

Annales Ordinis S. Benedicti, Sublaci, 1893-

Berger, E., *Les Registres d'Innocent IV*, 4 vols., Paris, 1884-1897.

Bizzarri, A., *Collectanea in Usum Secretariae Sacrae Congregationis Episcoporum et Regularium*, Romae, 1885.

Bruns, H. T., *Canones Apostolorum et Conciliorum Saeculorum IV-VII*, 2 vols., Berolini, 1839.

Bullarii Romani Continuatio Summorum Pontificum, 19 vols., Prati, 1756-1883.

Bullarum Diplomatum et Privilegiorum Sanctorum Romanorum Pontificum Taurinensis Editio, 24 vols. et Appendix, Augustae Taurinorum, 1857-1872.

Butler, C., *Sancti Benedicti Regula Monasteriorum*, 2. ed., Friburgi, Brisgoviae, 1927.

Canones et Decreta Sacrosancti Oecumenici Concilii Tridentini, Parisiis, 1856.

Codex Iuris Canonici Pii X Pontificis Maximi iussu digestus, Benedicti Papae XV auctoritate promulgatus, Romae, 1917.

Codicis Iuris Canonici Fontes cura Emi Card. Gasparri editi, 9 vols., Romae (postea Civitate Vaticana): Typis Polyglottis Vaticanis, 1923-1939. (Vols. VII-IV cura et studio Emi Card. Serédi.)

Corpus Iuris Canonici, 2. ed. Lipsiensis, post Aemilii Richteri curas instruxit Aemilius Friedberg, 2 vols., Lipsiae, 1879-1881.

Corpus Iuris Civilis, Vol. III, *Novellae*, ed. 5, stereotypa recognovit Schoell, absolvit Guglielmus Kroll, Berolini, 1928.

Corpus Scriptorum Ecclesiasticorum Latinorum, editum consilio et impensis Academiae Litterarum Caesariae Vindobonensis (*Corpus Vindobonense*), Vindobonae, 1866-

Decreta Authentica Congregationis Sacrorum Rituum, 5 vols. et 2 Appendices, Romae, 1898-1927.

Decretales D. Gregorii IX, una cum Glossis Restitutae, Romae, 1582.

Decretum Gratiani emendatum et notationibus illustratum, una cum Glossis, Gregorii XIII Pont. Max. iussu editum, 2 vols., Romae, 1582.

De Meester, P., *De Monachico Statu iuxta Disciplinam Byzantinam*, Codificazione Canonica Orientale, *Fonti*, Serie II, Fascicolo X, Civitate Vaticana: Typis Polyglottis Vaticanis, 1942.

Denzinger, H., Bannwart, C., Umberg, J. B., *Enchiridion Symbolorum, Definitionum, et Declarationum de Rebus Fidei et Morum,* 21.-23. ed., Friburgi Brisgoviae: Herder, 1937.

Ewald, P., Hartmann, L., *Gregorii I Papae Registrum Epistolarum, Monumenta Germaniae Historica,* Epistolarum Tomus I et II, Berolini, 1891-1899.

Jaffé, P., *Regesta Pontificum Romanorum ab condita Ecclesia ad annum post Christum natum MCXCVIII,* 2. ed. curaverunt S. Loewenfeld, F. Kaltenbrunner, P. Ewald, 2 vols., Lipsiae, 1885-1888.

Kozman, F., *Textes Legislatifs touchant le Cenobitisme Egyptien,* Codificazione Canonica Orientale, *Fonti,* Serie II, Fascicolo I, Civitate Vaticana: Typographie Polyglotte Vaticane, 1935.

Liber Sextus Decretalium D. Bonifacii Papae VIII suae integritati una Clementinis et Extravagantibus earumque Glossis restitutis, Romae, 1582.

Mansi, I., *Sacrorum Conciliorum Nova et Amplissima Collectio,* 53 vols. in 60, Paris, 1901-1927.

Martin, E., *Les Registres de Martin IV,* Paris, 1901.

Pallottini, S., *Collectio Omnium Conclusionum et Resolutionum Quae in Causis Propositis apud Sacram Congregationem Cardinalium S. Concilii Tridentini Interpretum Prodierunt ab Eius Institutione Anno MDLXIV ad Annum MDCCCLX, Distinctis Titulis Alphabetico Ordine per Materias Digesta,* 18 vols., Romae, 1868-1895.

Pontificale Romanum, Summorum Pontificum iussu editum, a Benedicto XIV et Leone XIII Pont. Max. recognitum et castigatum, Ratisbonae, 1908.

Potthast, A., *Regesta Pontificum Romanorum inde ab anno post Christum natum MCXCVIII ad annum MCCCIV,* 2 vols., Berolini, 1874-1875.

Rituale Monasticum, Collegeville, Minn.: Typis Abbatiae Sancti Joannis Baptistae, 1942.

Thesaurus Resolutionum Sacrae Congregationis Concilii, 167 vols., Romae, 1718-1908.

United States Code, 1940 ed., 4 vols., Washington, D. C.: United States Government Printing Office, 1941.

Waddingus, L., *Annales Minorum,* ed. nova, 25 vols., Ad Claras Aquas, 1931-1934.

Authors

Andre, M.-Wagner, J., *Dictionnaire de Droit Canonique,* 13. ed., 4 vols., Paris, 1901.

Appeltern, V., *Compendium Praelectionum Juris Regularis,* 2. ed., Parisiis, 1913.

Augustine, C., *A Commentary on the New Code of Canon Law,* 3. ed., 8 vols., St. Louis, Mo.: Herder, 1920-1931.

———, *Rights and Duties of Ordinaries according to the Code and Apostolic Faculties,* St. Louis, Mo., 1924.

Barbosa, A., *De Officio et Potestate Episcopi,* 2 vols., Lugduni, 1656.

Benedictus XIV (Prosper de Lambertinis), *De Synodo Diocesana,* 2 vols., Romae, 1806.

———, *Institutiones Ecclesiasticae,* Romae, 1747.

Benko, M., *The Abbot* NULLIUS, The Catholic University of America Canon Law Studies, n. 173, Washington, D. C.: The Catholic University of America Press, 1943.

Beste, U., *Introductio in Codicem,* 3. ed., Collegeville, Minn.: St. John's Abbey Press, 1946.

Blat, A., *Commentarium Textus Codicis Iuris Canonici,* 5 vols. in 7, Romae, 1921-1927.

Bolduc, G., *Les Études dans les Religions Cléricales,* The Catholic University of America Canon Law Studies, n. 149, Washington, D. C.: The Catholic University of America Press, 1942.

Bouix, D., *Tractatus de Jure Regularium,* 2 vols., Parisiis, 1857.

Bouscaren, T. L., *The Canon Law Digest,* 2 vols., Milwaukee: Bruce, 1934-1943.

Canavan, W., *The Profession of Faith,* The Catholic University of America Canon Law Studies, n. 151, Washington, D. C.: The Catholic University of America Press, 1942.

Capobianco, P., *Privilegia et Facultates Ordinis Fratrum Minorum,* Salerno: Ex Conventu S. M. Angelorum, 1946.

Cappello, F., *Summa Iuris Canonici,* Vols. I-II, 4. ed., 1945; Vol. III, 2. ed., 1940, 3 vols., Romae: Apud Aedes Universitatis Gregorianae.

———, *Tractatus Canonico-Moralis de Censuris,* 3. ed., Romae: Marietti, 1933.

———, *Tractatus Canonico-Moralis de Sacramentis,* Vol. IV, *De Sacra Ordinatione,* 2. ed., Taurini-Romae: Marietti, 1947.

Chelodi, I., *Ius Poenale,* Tridenti, 1925.

Coronata, M. Conte a, *De Sacramentis Tractatus Canonicus,* 3 vols., Taurini-Romae: Marietti, 1943-1946.

———, *Institutiones Iuris Canonici,* 2. ed., 5 vols., Taurini-Romae, Marietti, 1939-1947.

Coussa, A., *Epitome Praelectionum de Iure Ecclesiastico Orientali,* 2 vols., Vol. II, Venetiis: Typis Polyglottis Insulae S. Lazari, 1941.

Diederichs, M., *The Jurisdiction of the Latin Ordinaries over their Oriental Subjects,* The Catholic University of America Canon Law Studies, n. 229, Washington, D. C.: The Catholic University of America Press, 1946.

Fagnanus, P., *Commentaria in Quinque Libros Decretalium,* 5 vols., Coloniae Allobrogum, 1759.

Fanfani, L., *De Iure Religiosorum Ad Normam Codicis Iuris Canonici*, 2. ed., Taurini-Romae, 1925.

Ferraris, L., *Prompta Bibliotheca Canonica, Iuridica, Moralis, Theologica, necnon Ascetica, Polemica, Rubricistica, Historica*, ed. noviss., 9 vols., Romae, 1885-1899.

Gallagher, T., *The Examination of the Qualities of the Ordinand*, The Catholic University of America Canon Law Studies, n. 195, Washington, D. C.: The Catholic University of America Press, 1944.

Gannon, J., *The Interstices Required for the Promotion to Orders*, The Catholic University of America Canon Law Studies, n. 196, Washington, D. C.: The Catholic University of America Press, 1944.

Gasparri, P., *Tractatus Canonicus de Sacra Ordinatione*, 2 vols., Parisiis, 1893-1894.

Gill, N., *The Spiritual Prefect in Clerical Houses of Study*, The Catholic University of America Canon Law Studies, n. 216, Washington, D. C.: The Catholic University of America Press, 1945.

Gonzales-Tellez, Manuel, *Commentaria Perpetua in Singulos Textus Quinque Librorum Decretalium Gregorii IX*, 5 vols., Venetiis, 1699.

Hallier, F., *De Sacris Electionibus et Ordinationibus ex Antiquo et Novo Ecclesiae Usu*, in Migne, J. P., *Theologiae Cursus Completus*, Vol. XXIV, Parisiis, 1860.

Hickey, J., *Irregularities and Simple Impediments in the New Code of Canon Law*, The Catholic University of America Canon Law Studies, n. 7, Washington, D. C.: The Catholic University of America, 1920.

Honorante, R., *Praxis Secretariae Tribunalis Cardinalis Urbis Vicarii*, 2. ed., Romae, 1762.

Hynes, H., *The Privileges of Cardinals*, The Catholic University of America Canon Law Studies, n. 217, Washington: D. C.: The Catholic University of America Press, 1945.

Jorio, D., *Sacerdos Alter Christus: De Instructione pro Scrutinio ad Ordines Peragendo Commentarius*, Romae: Sindacato Italiano Arti Grafiche, 1933.

Kurtscheid, B., *Historia Iuris Canonici, Historia Institutorum*, Vol. I, *Ab Ecclesiae Fundatione usque ad Gratianum*, Romae: Officium Libri Catholici, 1941.

Langasco, A. a, *De Institutione Clericorum in Disciplinis Inferioribus*, Romae: Typis Polyglottis Vaticanis, 1936.

Leurenius, P., *Forum Ecclesiasticum*, 5 vols., Venetiis, 1729.

Mabillon, I., *Annales Ordinis S. Benedicti*, 6 vols., Lucase, 1739-1745.

———, *Tractatus de Studiis Monasticis*, 3 vols., Venetiis, 1745.

Many, S., *Praelectiones de Sacra Ordinatione*, Parisiis, 1905.

Migne, J. P., *Patrologiae Cursus Completus, Series Graeca*, 161 vols., Parisiis, 1857-1866.

———, *Patrologiae Cursus Completus, Series Latina*, 221 vols., Parisiis, 1844-1864.

Molitor, R., *Religiosi Iuris Capita Selecta,* Romae, 1909.

Monacelli, F., *Formularium Legale Practicum Fori Ecclesiastici,* 3 vols., Venetiis, 1736-1751.

Morinus, I., *Commentarius de Sacris Ecclesiae Ordinationibus,* Parisiis, 1655.

Nabuco, J., *Pontificalis Romani Expositio Juridico-Practica,* 3 vols., Petropoli: Editôra Vozes Ltda., 1945.

O'Brien, J., *The Exemption of Religious in Church Law,* Milwaukee: Bruce, 1942.

Oesterle, G., *Praelectiones Iuris Canonici* (manuscripti instar), Vol. I, Romae: Collegio S. Anselmi, 1931.

Passerinus, P. F., *De Hominum Statibus et Officiis,* 3 vols., Lucae, 1732.

Pejška, J., *Ius Canonicum Religiosorum,* 3. ed., Friburgi Brisgoviae, 1927.

Petra, V., *Commentaria ad Constitutiones Apostolicas,* 5 vols., Venetiis, 1729.

Petrani, A., *De Relatione Iuridica inter Diversos Ritus in Ecclesia Catholica,* Romae: Marietti, 1930.

Piat, F., *Praelectiones Iuris Regularis,* 3. ed., 3 vols., Tornaci, 1905.

Pignatelli, I., *Consultationes Canonicae,* 17 vols., Coloniae Allobrogum, 1700.

Prümmer, D., *Manuale Iuris Canonici,* 6. ed., Friburgi Brisgoviae: Herder, 1933.

Regatillo, E., *Institutiones Iuris Canonici,* 2 vols., Santander: Sal Terrae, 1941-1942.

———, *Ius Sacramentarium,* 2 vols., Santander: Sal Terrae, 1946.

Riganti, I., *Commentaria in Regulas, Constitutiones, et Ordinationes Cancellariae Apostolicae,* 4 vols., Coloniae Allobrogum, 1751.

Sartori, C., *Jurisprudentiae Ecclesiasticae Elementa,* Romae: Pontif. Athenaeum Antonianum, 1946.

Schaefer, T., *De Religiosis Ad Normam Codicis Iuris Canonici,* 4. ed., Romae: Editrice "Apostolico Cattolico," 1947.

Schmalzgrueber, F., *Jus Ecclesiasticum Universum,* 5 vols. in 12, Romae, 1843-1845.

Shuhler, R., *Privileges of Regulars to Absolve and Dispense,* The Catholic University of America Canon Law Studies, n. 186, Washington, D. C.: The Catholic University of America Press, 1943.

Sipos, S., *Enchiridion Iuris Canonici,* 4. ed., Pécs: Ex Typographia "Haladás R. T.," 1940.

Tamburini, A., *De Jure Abbatum et Aliorum Praelatorum tam Regularium quam Secularium Episcopis Inferiorum,* 3 vols., Coloniae Agrippinae, 1691.

Thomassinus, L., *Vetus et Nova Ecclesiae Disciplina,* 10 vols., Magontiaci, 1787.

Toso, A., *Ad Codicem Iuris Canonici Commentaria Minora,* 5 vols., Romae, 1920-1927.

Van Espen, B., *Jus Ecclesiasticum Universum,* 10 vols., Venetiis, 1769.

Vermeersch, A.-Creusen, J., *Epitome Iuris Canonici,* 6. ed., 3 vols., Mechlinae-Romae: Dessain, 1937-1946.

Vogelpohl, H., *The Simple Impediments to Holy Orders,* The Catholic University of America Canon Law Studies, n. 223, Washington, D. C.: The Catholic University of America Press, 1945.

Wernz, F., *Ius Decretalium,* 6 vols., Romae, 1898-1905.

Wernz- F.-Vidal, P., *Ius Canonicum,* 7 vols. in 9, Romae: Apud Aedes Universitatis Gregorianae, 1923-1938.

ARTICLES

(Anonymous), "De Ordinatione a Proprio Superiore Religioso"—*Periodica,* XII (1923), (163)-(164).

———, "De Ordinatione Religiosorum, quod ad Episcopum Proprium"—*Periodica,* XIV (1925), (52)-(53).

———, "Use of Pontificals by Benedictine Abbots"—*ER,* CVIII (1943), 454-456.

Beck, E., "Two Bulls of Boniface IX for the Abbot of St. Osyth"—*The English Historical Review,* XXVI (1911), 125-127.

Chamard, F., "Les Abbés au Moyen Age"—*Revue des Questions Historiques,* XXXVIII (1885), 71-108.

Coronata, M. Conte a, "Pene e Procedimenti 'ad modum praecepti' "—*Perfice Munus!* VII (1932), 353-354.

Creusen, J., "Admission d'Orientaux au Noviciat"—*Revue des Communautés Religieuses,* II (1926), 41.

De Antoñana, M., "Consultationes"—*CpR,* V (1924), 226-228.

Frison, B., "Ex-Seminarian and Novice: A Clarification"—*The Jurist,* VI (1946), 416-418.

Gerland, M., "Le Ministre Extraordinaire du Sacrement de l'Ordre"—*Revue Thomiste,* XXXVI (1931), 874-885.

Gómez, M., "De Abbatum Potestate Tonsuram Minoresque Ordines Conferendi"—*CpR,* IX (1928), 434-446; X (1929), 45-52.

Goyeneche, S., "Consultationes"—*CpR,* I (1920), 227-228.

———, "Consultationes"—*CpR,* III (1922), 264.

———, "Consultationes"—*CpR,* V (1924), 164-165.

———, "Consultationes"—*CpRM,* XVIII (1937), 94-95.

Hugon, E., "Etudes Recentes sur le Sacrement de l'Ordre"—*Revue Thomiste,* XXIX (1924), 490-493.

La Puma, V., "Adnotationes"—*CpRM,* XXIII (1942), 226-237.

Larraona, A., "Commentarium Codicis"—*CpRM,* XVIII (1937), 149-150.

———, "Commentarium Codicis"—*CpRM,* XXV (1944-1946), 24-25.

Ledwolorz, A., "De Regularium Privilegiis Recipiendi Sacros Ordines extra Tempora et Non Servatis Interstitiis"—*Antonianum,* XX (1945), 427-438.

Noval, I., "De Ratione Corrigendi ac Puniendi"—*Jus Pontificium,* III (1923), 208-210.

Oesterle, G., "De Potestate Superiorum Maiorum in Religionibus Clercalibus Exemptis"—*CpRM,* XXV (1944-1946), 39-47.

———, "De Ratione Studiorum in Religionibus Clericalibus"—*CpR,* V (1924), 444-460; VI (1925), 34-42, 141-146, 191-202, 296-323.

Pistocchi, M., "De Superiore Potestatem Coactivam Habente"—*Il Monitore Ecclesiastico,* IL (1937), 38-39.

Schaaf, V., "Episcopus Proprius Ordinationis Religiosorum"—*ER,* XC (1934), 497-498.

Vermeersch, A., "Annotationes"—*Periodica,* V (1911), 210.

———, "Annotationes"—*Periodica,* V (1911), 272.

———, "Annotationes"—*Periodica,* VI (1912), 27.

———, "Canon 542, 2°, et Dispensatio ab Irregularitate"—*Periodica,* XX (1931), 136*-137*.

Villien, A., "L'Ordination"—*Le Canoniste Contemporaine,* XLV (1922), 104-105, 196.

Voltas, P., "Consultationes"—*CpR,* II (1921), 369.

———, "De Domicilio quoad Ordinationem Religiosorum"—*CpR,* II (1921), 301-302.

PERIODICALS

Antonianum, Romae, 1926-

Canoniste Contemporaine, Le, Parisiis, 1878-1922; 1924-1926, *Le Canoniste.*

Commentarium pro Religiosis, Romae, 1920-1934; 1935, *Commentarium pro Religiosis et Missionariis.*

Ecclesiastical Review, The, Philadelphia, 1889-1943; *The American Ecclesiastical Review,* Washington, 1944-

English Historical Review, The, London, 1886-

Jurist, The, Washington, D. C., 1941-

Jus Pontificium, Romae, 1921-

Monitore Ecclesiastico, Il, Romae, 1876-

Perfice Munus! Taurini, 1926-

Periodica de Religiosis et Missionariis, Brugis, 1905-1919; *Periodica de Re Canonica et Morali utili praesertim Religiosis et Missionariis,* 1920-1927; *Periodica de Re Canonica, Morali, Liturgica,* 1927-

Revue des Communautés Religieuses, Louvain, 1925-

Revue des Questions Historiques, Paris, 1866-

Revue Thomiste, Paris, 1893-

ABBREVIATIONS

AAS—*Acta Apostolicae Sedis*
ASS—*Acta Sanctae Sedis*
CpR, CpRM—*Commentarium pro Religiosis et Missionariis*
CSEL—*Corpus Scriptorum Ecclesiasticorum Latinorum*
ER—*The Ecclesiastical Review*
N.—*Corpus Iuris Civilis, Novellae*
P.C.I.—Pontificia Commissio ad Codicis Canones Authentice Interpretandos
PG—Migne, *Patrologiae Cursus Completus, Series Graeca*
PL—Migne, *Patrologiae Cursus Completus, Series Latina*
S. C. C.—Sacra Congregatio Concilii
S. C. Consist.—Sacra Congregatio Consistorialis
S. C. de Prop. Fide—Sacra Congregatio de Propaganda Fide
S. C. Ep. et Reg.—Sacra Congregatio Episcoporum et Regularium
S. C. pro Eccl. Or.—Sacra Congregatio pro Ecclesia Orientali
S. C. S. Off.—Sacra Congregatio Sancti Officii
S. R. C.—Sacra Congregatio Sacrorum Rituum
S. R. R.—Sacra Romana Rota

BIOGRAPHICAL NOTE

Maur John Dlouhy was born in Chicago, Illinois, on March 21, 1919. After attending St. Procopius (Chicago) and Our Lady of the Holy Mount (Cicero) parochial schools, he entered the Academy and later the College conducted by the Benedictine Fathers of St. Procopius Abbey at Lisle, Illinois. In 1938 he entered the novitiate for that abbey, and upon professing in 1939, continued his philosophical and theological studies at the Seminary of that Abbey. On receiving his Bachelor of Arts degree in 1941, he registered for graduate studies in economics at the Catholic University of America in Washington. He was ordained to the priesthood in 1944, and the following year enrolled in the School of Canon Law at that University, where he received the degrees of Bachelor and Licentiate of Canon Law in 1946 and 1947.

ALPHABETICAL INDEX

www.ingramcontent.com/pod-product-compliance
Lightning Source LLC
LaVergne TN
LVHW050217080826
844660LV00012B/429

* 9 7 8 0 8 1 3 2 2 4 4 9 7 *